WOMEN AND CHILD TRAFFICKING IN INDIA

WOMEN AND CHILD TRAFFICKING IN INDIA

A Human Right Perspective

Dr. REKHA ROY

AKANSHA PUBLISHING HOUSE
NEW DELHI • GUWAHATI • VISAKHAPATNAM

AKANSHA PUBLISHING HOUSE
4649-B/21, Ansari Road
Daryaganj, New Delhi-110002
Phones: 23268193, 09435116718
Email: ektabooks@yahoo.com
visit us: www.akanshapublishinghouse.com

Women and Child Trafficking in India: A Human Right Perspective

First Published 2010

ISBN 978-81-8370-253-9

PRINTED IN INDIA

Published by Akansha Publishing House, New Delhi-110002 and printed at Harmain Offset Press, Delhi.

Contents

Acknowledgements

Trafficking in women and children is the most-abominable violation of human rights. Women and children were becoming vulnerable to trafficking as they were unable to survive with dignity because of lack of livelihood options. In the absence of awareness of human rights, the economically and socially deprived people at the grassroots have become easy prey to the trafficking trade. The crime of trafficking involves the violation of a whole gamut of laws and human rights. It becomes a threat to society because traffickers operate across borders with impunity, with the growing involvement of organized criminals and by generally undermining the rule of law. Trafficking 'threatens' the very fabric of society because it involves not only criminals but also law enforcing agencies. Trafficking in women and children is a violation of several human rights including the very right to life, the right to liberty and human dignity and security of person, the right to freedom from torture or cruelty, inhuman or degrading treatment, the right to a home and family, the right to education and proper employment, the right to healthcare and everything that makes for a life with dignity. To address the issue of human trafficking in a holistic and right based manner. By this I mean a correct and sensitive approach that takes into account several aspects such as right to life; right to security; right to privacy; access to health services; right to self-determination of the trafficked person and addresses the core issue of prevention and protection so as to bring about a determined effort to prevent trafficking.

As such, I am extremely grateful to all who helped me to complete the research and prepare the final output for publication. I am deeply indebted to my husband, Mr Pranesh Roy, who constantly and affectionately prodded me to complete the work up to the stage of preparing this manuscript for publication. I also would like to acknowledge my little son Parash who unhappily missed me when I was involved in research. My thanks are also due to Mr. Pradip Debnath for typing the final manuscript. My publishers Mr. M.P. Misra of Akansha Publishing House, New Delhi, deserve a special note of thanks.

—Dr. Rekha Roy

1

Introduction

Human trafficking is the commerce and trade in the movement or migration of people, legal and illegal, including both legitimate labour activities as well as forced labour. The term is used in a more narrow sense by advocacy groups to mean the recruitment, transportation, harbouring, or receipt of people for the purposes of slavery, prostitution, forced labour (including bonded labour or debt bondage) and servitude. Trafficking in persons as the recruitment, transportation, transfer, harbouring receipt of persons, by means of the threat or use of force or other forms of coercion, of abduction, of fraud, of deception, of the abuse of power or of a position of vulnerability or of giving or receiving of payments or benefits to achieve the consent of a person having control over another person, for the purpose of exploitation. Exploitation includes forcing people into prostitution or other forms of sexual exploitation, forced labour or services, slavery, or practices similar to slavery and servitude. For children, exploitation may also include forced prostitution, illicit international adoption, trafficking for early marriage, or recruitments as child soldiers, beggars, for sports (such as child camel jockey or football players), or within certain religious groups.[1]

Human trafficking differs from people smuggling. In the latter, people voluntarily request the smuggler's service for fees, and there may be no deception involved in the (illegal) agreement. On arrival at their destination, the smuggled person is usually freed. On the other hand, the trafficking victim is enslaved, or the terms of their debt bondage are highly exploitative. The trafficker takes away the basic human rights of the victim.[2] Victims are sometime tricked and lured by false promises or are physically forced.[3] Some traffickers use coercive and manipulative tactics including deception, intimidation, feigned love, isolation, threat and use of physical force, and debt bondage.[4] People who are seeking entry to other countries may be picked up by traffickers and misled into thinking that they will be free after being smuggled across the border. In some cases, they are captured through slave raiding, although this is increasingly rare.

Trafficked people are usually the most vulnerable and powerless minorities in a region. They often come from the poorer areas where opportunities are limited, they often are ethnic minorities, and, they often are displaced persons such as runaways or refugees, though they may come from any social background, class or race.

Trafficking in women and children is the gravest form of abuse and exploitation of human beings. Women are particularly at risk from sex trafficking. Criminals exploit lack of opportunities for study, and then force the victims to become prostitutes. Through agents and brokers who arrange the travel and job placements, women are escorted to their destinations and delivered to the employers. Upon reaching their destinations, some women learn that they have been deceived about the nature of the work they will do; most have been lied about the financial arrangement and conditions of their employment and find themselves in coercive or abusive situations from which escape is both difficult and dangerous.

Trafficking in human beings take place for the purpose of exploitation which in general could be categorised as (a) Sex-based and (b) Non-sex based. The former category includes trafficking for prostitution, commercial sexual abuse, pedephilia, pornography, cyber sex, and different types of disguised sexual exploitation that take place in some of the massage parlor, beauty parlors, bars and other manifestations like call girls racket, friends clubs etc. Non sex based trafficking could be for different types of servitude, like domestic labour, industrial labour, adoption, organ transplant, camel racing, marriage related rackets etc. But the growing traffic in women is principally for the purpose of prostitution is an international problem which can be found in both developing and industrialized nations. Unfortunately, society remains tolerant of this abominable crime against women. There are ways of getting women into prostitution that are common to many countries: then there are particular methods unique to a country. Probably the three most common methods are false employment promises, false marriages and kidnapping. But what makes women and girls vulnerable are economic distress, desertion by their spouses, sexually exploitative social customs and family traditions.

According to a recent survey women are bought and sold with impunity and trafficked at will to other countries from different parts of India. These girls and women are sourced from Dindigal, Madurai, Tiruchirapalli and Chengalpattu in Tamil Nadu; Gaya, Kishanganj, Patna, Katihar, Purnea, Araria and Madhubani from Bihar; Murshidabad and 24 Parganas in West Bengal; Maharaigunj from UP; Dholpur, Alwar, Tonk from Rajasthan; Mangalore, Gulbarga and Raichur from Karnataka. These women and girls are supplied to Thailand, Kenya, South Africa and Middle East countries like Bahrain; Dubai; Oman; Britain; South Korea and Philippines. They are forced to work as sex workers undergoing severe exploitation and abuse. These women are the most vulnerable group in contracting HIV infection. Due to unrelenting poverty and lack of unemployment opportunities there is an increase in the voluntary entry of women into sex work.

Trafficking both for commercial sexual exploitation and for non-sex based exploitation is a transnational and complex challenge as it is an organized criminal activity, and extreme form of economic empowerment and social justice. The trafficking of women and children causes untold miseries as it violates the rights and dignity of the individual in several ways. It violates the individual's right to life, dignity, security, privacy, health, education and redressal of grievances.

All is not well with children in India's Northeast. A study conducted by a Guwahati based NGO along with the police has revealed that a shocking 20 percent involved in prostitution in the region are aged between 11 and 17 years. In addition, the report also states that most of the children are victims of acute physical torture. "They are initially raped and flogged almost to death to take up the profession", the report said. Almost half of the child prostitutes were from Assam, followed by Meghalaya, Manipur, Tripura, Nagaland, Mizoram and Arunachal Pradesh. Every year thousands of the tea tribe girls are lured by people and taken to different parts of India, to work as slave and in most of the cases they lands up in brothels. Those who are forced into sex work, or who are vulnerable to sexual exploitation as domestic labourers, are particularly at risk of sexual transmitted infections, including HIV and unwanted pregnancy. The plight of the women from this community has remained unheard and unattended, since ages and they have no other options but to migrate and to follow the people who lure them and assure them good jobs outside the state.

Trafficking of children often involves exploitation of the parents' extreme poverty. Parents may sell children to traffickers in order to pay off debts of gain income, or they may be deceived concerning the prospects of training and a better life for their children. Poverty, often cited as a major reason responsible for trafficking in children is not the only cause. Loss of traditional sources of livelihood, growing unemployment, forced migration, the commodification of children and growing consumerism resulting from globalization have all contributed to the increase in child trafficking. The socio-economic situation and geographical location of the family add to the vulnerability. While both boys and girls are victims of trafficking, girls are more vulnerable, especially to trafficking for sexual purposes. Anecdotal evidence suggests that the outlawed religious practices like the 'Devdasi' and 'Jogin' systems, temple priests have used their position to traffic girls for prostitution. Traffickers sell girls to the Bedia and Bacohara communities who live in Madhya Pradesh, and the border district of Uttar Pradesh and Maharashtra and to the Rajnats of Rajasthan, families where prostitution is traditional means of earning a livelihood.

India shares a porous border with over seven countries all of which is not fenced. With the connivance of border police on either side, it is not difficult to enter India. Political instability and economic compulsions are reason for young girls from Nepal, Bangladesh, Myanmar and even as far Uzbekistan, to be sold to traffickers. Trafficking from these countries is one way route, 'into India'.

Human trafficking is not a stand alone issue. It is closely related to other issues that threaten security well being of the victims. Victims are exposed to continuous threats of physical violence by traffickers to ensure compliance. Many are held in bondage and beaten to suppress resistance. Other threats includes absolute poverty due to wage deprivation. They are unprotected by labour laws, and long working hours as well as lack of holiday is common.

There is no universally accepted definition of trafficking for sexual exploitation. The term encompasses the organized movement of people, usually women, between countries and within countries for sex work with the use of physical coercion, deception and bondage through forced debt. However, the issue becomes contentious when the element of coercion is removed from the definition to incorporate facilitating the willing involvement in prostitution Save the Children stated "The issue gets mired in controversy and confusion when prostitution itself is considered as a violation of the basic human rights of both adult women and minors, and equal to sexual exploitation per se ... trafficking and prostitution become conflated with each other ... on account of the historical conflation of trafficking and prostitution both legally and in popular understanding, an overwhelming degree of effort and interventions of anti-trafficking groups are concentrated on trafficking into prostitution.[5]

Sexual Trafficking includes coercing a migrant into a sexual act as a condition of allowing or arranging the migration. Sexual trafficking uses physical coercion, deception and bondage incurred through forced debt. Trafficked women and children, for instance, are often promised work in the domestic or service industry, but instead are usually taken to brothels where their passports and other identification papers are confiscated. They may be beaten or locked up and promised their freedom only after earning through prostitution – their purchase price, as well as their travel and visa costs.[6] The main motive of a woman (in some cases an underage girl) to accept an offer from a trafficker is better financial opportunities for herself or her family. In many cases traffickers initially offer 'legitimate' work or the promise of an opportunity to study. The main type of work offered are in the catering and hotel industry, in bars and clubs, modeling contacts etc. Trafficking sometimes use offers of marriage, threats, intimidation and kidnapping as means of obtaining victims. In the majority of cases, the women end up in prostitution. Also some (migrating) prostitutes become victims of human trafficking. Some women know they will be working as prostitutes, but they have an inaccurate view of the circumstances and the conditions of the work in their country of destination.[7] In Japan the prosperous entertainment market had created huge demand for commercial sexual workers, and such demand is being met by trafficking women and children from Philippines, Colombia and Thailand. Women are forced into street prostitution, besed stripping and live sex acts.[8]

The Fundamentalist Church of Jesus Christ of Latter Day Saints, (not to be confused with the Church of Jesus Christ of Latter Day Saints) in the US and Canada, has also been implicated in the trafficking of underage women across state lines and international borders (US/Canada). In most cases this is for the continuation of polygamous practices, in the form of plural marriage.[9]

Trafficking victims are also exposed to different psychological problems. They suffer social alienation in the host and home countries. Stigmatization, social exclusion and intolerance make reintegration into local communities difficult. The government offer little assistance and social services to trafficked victims upon their return. As the victims are also pushed into drug trafficking, many of them face criminal sanctions.

Trafficking in human beings especially in women and children has become a matter of serious national and international concern. Women and children - boys and girls - have been exposed to unprecedented vulnerabilities. Commercial exploitation of these vulnerabilities has become a massive organized crime and a multimillion dollar business. Nations are attempting to combat this trade in human misery through legislative, executive, judicial and social action.

In India too, over the last decade, the volume of human trafficking has increased. Though the exact numbers are not known, it is one of the most lucrative criminal trades, next to arms and drug smuggling undertaken by highly organized criminals. In spite of the magnitude of the problem, India has not put in place appropriate measures to tackle human trafficking. The Indian constitution prohibits human trafficking and successive governments have formulated laws intended to tackle it, with the primary legislative too being the Immoral Traffic (Prevention) Act 1956. However these laws are either weak or inadequately enforced. The combination of the lack of infrastructure and resources, in conjunction with the powerful political and business connections of the traffickers, means that the laws are inadequately enforced. In addition, in practical terms the victims of trafficking suffer disproportionately under the law; four times as many women as men are arrested under the legislation intended to tackle human trafficking thus effectively criminalizing the victims. Article 23 of the constitution of India prohibits trafficking in any form. We have special legislations like Immoral Traffic Prevention Act (ITPA), 1956, the Bonded Labour System (Abolition) Act, 1976 and the Juvenile Justice (Care and Protection) Act 2000. the law enforcement scenario seen from the traditional viewpoint, presents a dismal picture, which I am going to discuss in succeedung chapters. Despite being an affected country, India lacks in efforts to enforce law to tackle human trafficking of men, women and children. Despite presence of many framework, there is a need to enforce such laws to curb trafficking from and into India. Not only enforcing laws but there is also need to develop the areas, which serve as a source for human trafficking. The root cause of the problem is poverty, under development, unemployment among others. Therefore there is a need to address the problem both socially and by enforcing laws. Some of these major problems and issues will be discussed in the succeeding chapters.

NOTES & REFERENCES

1. Uefa.com

2. Distinguishing between Human Trafficking and People Smuggling. UN Office on Drugs and Crime.

3. Local women fall prey to sex slavery abroad.

4. Trafficking in human being.

5. Definition of Trafficking - Save the Children Nepal.

6. Migration Information Programme Trafficking and Prostitution: the growing exploitation of migrant women from Central and Eastern Europe, Geneva International Organization for Migration, 1995.

7. Research based on case studies of victims of trafficking in human being in 3EU member states, i.e. Belgium, Italy and The Netherlands, Commission of European communities, D G Justice and Home Affairs 2001, http://www.prostitute/studie/documentes/mensenhandetresearchcasestraffic.pdf, retrieved 2008-10-05.

8. Dinan K. Owed justice: Thai women trafficked into debt bondage in Japan. New York, NY, Human Rights Watch, 2000

9. Robert Motos, where 'the handsome ones go to the leaders' May 3, 2008, Globe and Mail and Daniel Woods, Bountiful, B.C. August 4, 2001. ricross.com

2

Women and Child Trafficking: Literature Review

The available literature on trafficking mainly consists of reports of studies, conferences and workshops conducted by international and domestic non-governmental organisations (NGOs). National and regional level studies are fewer in number compared to the literature available at the state level. The recent importance accorded to trafficking on the international agenda is responsible for the rise in the number of ongoing research studies on trafficking in India.

Though not exhaustive, the current review explores various perspectives and debates, positions and conclusions on trafficking in women and children. It is organised around the major themes that emerged from the literature—the definition of trafficking, the various stages of the operation and the anti-trafficking initiatives in India—while keeping in mind the objectives of the Action Research on Trafficking in Women and Children (ARTWAC).

The Indian Constitution prohibits all forms of trafficking under Article 23. The Suppression of the Immoral Traffic Act, 1956 (amended to the Immoral Traffic Prevention Act) was in response to the ratification of the International Convention on Suppression of Immoral Traffic and Exploitation of Prostitution of Others in 1950 by India. Trafficking has been an area of concern since the early 20th century. It especially attracted attention during the 1980s. More recently, there has been a widening of its focus. However, this was not accompanied by an independent and sustained mass movement, against trafficking in the country (D'Cunha 1998).

The literature on trafficking devotes a considerable amount of space to defining the phenomenon. The numerous definitions available reflect the lack of clarity and consensus on what precisely constitutes trafficking. Over decades, the concept itself has evolved, to include many more attributes and features than it began with. So much so that 'increasingly, it has been recognised that historical characterisations of trafficking are outdated, ill-defined and non-responsive to the current realities of the movement and trade in people and to the nature and extent of the abuses inherent in and incidental to trafficking'. (United Nations 2000:8).

The various definitions reflect differences in the interpretation, understanding, emphasis, inclusion or exclusion of specific elements and attributes of trafficking. Debates, arguments and confusions appear to be centered around the issues of consent and movement; purpose relation with smuggling and illegal migration; and treatment of women and children.

The United Nations Protocol to Prevent, Suppress, and Punish Trafficking in Persons, Especially Women and Children adopted in November 2000, which is part of the United Nations Convention Against Organised Crime[1], 'provides the first internationally recognised' definition of trafficking (ESCAP 2003). Besides giving 'a framework for further discussions', it has proved to be a 'guiding principle for a macro conceptual understanding on trafficking' (UNIFEM 2003b).

This definition has expanded the exploitative conditions that may result from trafficking, which were earlier confined only to prostitution. Thus, it is considered to be more inclusive. The positive aspects of this definition are stated to be the elaboration of the means used, its clarity on the issue of consent (one of the most debated issues in trafficking)[2] and the different acts in the trafficking process that it encompasses. Concern has been expressed that the 'first modern definition of trafficking is being elaborated in the context of crime control, rather than with a focus on human rights' (United Nations 2000:7). It is also viewed as one which confuses the lay person (UNICEF 2001). Thus, the debate is continuing post-2000, with other definitions being suggested and adopted by Coomarswamy. [United Nations (2001), ILO-IPEC

(2001b:1) and SAARC (2001)]. A legal definition of trafficking has for the first time been attempted by the Goa Children's Act.

An explanation for this continued debate is that the 'concept of "trafficking" can easily be expanded, limited or shifted to accommodate institutional objectives and context' (ILO 2002a: 5). An ESCAP report has also concluded that trafficking is a multidimensional form of exploitation, wherein each dimension has its own legal and conceptual framework. There are multiple types of trafficking, each with different implications, yet part of 'an interrelated web of varying contexts'. Thus, any expectations of a universal consistency in definitions of trafficking seem unrealistic (ESCAP 2003). The viewpoint that regions and contexts influence the interpretation of the term is clearly reflected in the literature.

The multiplicity of attributes and variables involved in the trafficking process and the different perspectives on the subject is another reason for the wide variation in the suggested forms of trafficking. There is no uniform method of classifying these forms. For instance, some suggested forms are defined on the basis of differences at the place of origin; others focus on difference arising at the destinations; some make the methods adopted by traffickers as the basis of the forms; others use the criteria of purpose. (DWCD 1996; Friedman 2001: 4; HAQ Centre 2001; ILO 2001: 18; Marshall 2001; Mattar 2002; DePaul University 2002; IDS 2003).

In the literature surveyed there seems to be broad agreement over the factors that lead to trafficking. However, there is uncertainty about precise role played by them. While some reports view these factors to be the root causes of trafficking, others state that 'they merely exacerbate the vulnerability of marginalised and disadvantaged groups and render them increasingly more amenable to a variety of harm' (Sanghera 2002). These factors relate to the socio-economic and political contexts of people, are interlinked and may be divided into two categories—personal circumstances and structural forces that influence the context (Raymond et al. 2002; DePaul University 2002). They are generally listed in the context of commercial sexual exploitation. Mukherjee has identified 'fifty seven factors which play the role of causal agents to push women and girls towards prostitution' (SEVA 2003).

People with personal characteristics of low self-esteem and lack of self-control are reported to be vulnerable (UNDP 2002). Low levels of literacy, awareness and information are also risk factors. Economic depravation due to various reasons and its associative conditions are among the most important factors that lead to vulnerability. Almost all the studies and reports under review found that a high percentage of trafficked people belong to lower income groups. Greater the degree of impoverishment, higher is the risk of falling prey to trafficking (Mukherjee and Das, 1996; Warburton 1996; DWCD 1998; UNDP 2002). People with disabilities or women who may suffer from "disfigurements" are also vulnerable (Gathia 2003: 5)

A dysfunctional home environment—break-up of the family, marital discord, physical abuse, sexual abuse, drug use, family pressures, large families, families facing uncertain times, children in substitute care, gender discrimination within the family, desertion by husbands, husbands' acquiring a second or a third wife—makes people vulnerable to trafficking. Studies by CSWB and others have shown that most trafficked women were unmarried, divorced, separated or widowed (Karmakar 2001). The involvement of another family member in commercial sex work also creates vulnerability (Warburton and Maria, 1996).

Environments lacking livelihood options or economic opportunities, with the accompanying pressures to work and earn, make peoples' lives on ongoing 'battle for survival' (Sanghera 1999). The structural factors influencing and determining these circumstances are listed as industrialization and globalisations; economic crises, decline, disruption or underdevelopment; economic policies like privatisation, liberalisation, promotion of sex tourism, withdrawal of subsidies and commercialisation of agriculture; the consequent erosion of subsistence agricultural practices, loss of traditional livelihoods and inflation. Labour demand and policies also influence vulnerability. In a global market, women and girls are increasingly being hired as service providers, which puts them at risk (*ibid.*).

Some of the political factors listed are conflicts, disruption and instability; immigration policies, human rights violations, and the gaps between government rhetoric and practice. Poor governance, limited law enforcement or implementation of labour standards also create vulnerabilities (ADB 2002: 9). Environmental calamities and disruptions may also put people at risk.

The quickening pace of urbanisation and heightened mobility resulting from the development of road links are contributing factors. A culture of consumerism, materialism, commodification of individuals and commercialisation of sex distorts family needs and individual desires (NCW 1997; Raymond 2002). A mindset which judges children's worth by the amount of money they can earn, and how soon they are able to do so, has developed (ISS 2003b), justifying their exploitation by kin members. Discriminatory practices and social exclusion exacerbate the vulnerabilities of groups like Scheduled Tribes, Scheduled Castes, Other Backward Castes, ethnic minorities, tribal communities, undocumented migrant workers, stateless people or people in refugee camps.

The literature surveyed emphasises the fact that trafficking occurs in a wider context of increasing instances of human rights violation against women. These include the violation of their reproductive rights and the rights of female infants and foetuses to live; domestic violence against women, custodial violence against women, violence against women in markets and other public places; the violation of women's rights to decision-making and to land assets and other resources (Warburton and Maria, 1996; Sanghera 1999; Karmakar 2001; ADB 2002; Raymond et al). In 'cases where their families or guardians push women or girls into trafficked circumstances, many do not consider this as harmful, as they are considered chattels of their father or guardian and further protection from their community would be inappropriate' (ADB 2002: 15). Instances of male relatives making periodic visits to collect a girl's earnings have been reported (Nirmala Niketan, College of Social Work, 2003). Thus, there is a non-recognition and non-acceptance of such practices as being exploitative. Early marriage, lack of choice regarding marriage partner and their socialisation into women who remain servile and bear injustice silently are other factors that render them more vulnerable (ADB 2002: 42).

Sanghera (1999) elaborates how the feminisation of poverty and migration increases vulnerability to traffickers. Driven by the pressing need for gainful employment, with scarcity of jobs in their home bases, women and children are easy prey for the designs of unscrupulous agents, offering 'choices' and assistance with travel, particularly across borders, for jobs.

Vulnerable groups and their spatial or geographical locations have been analysed in relation to women. Though the list is not exhaustive, places where poor women in India (rural and urban) are located have been identified (DWCD 1996; Sanghera 1999; Murthy and Sankaran 2001). Contrary to the general perception, a study from Orissa found that 'developed areas with improved infrastructure have invariably been the source as well as the destination of trafficking in women', though in these areas 80 per cent of the population or victims still belonged to landless households and families dependent on wage labour for survival (Pandey, 2002). This suggests that a further examination of the spaces where there is an intersection of the affluent and the not-so-affluent may be needed to fully understand and explain vulnerability.

Street children and those living in slums; the orphaned and the disabled; children living in brothels or in communities practicing religious and cultural prostitution; children who have been stigmatised by abuse or molestation; children born to victims of AIDS; children in custodial and educational institutions away from families; and children of bonded labourers and those working as domestic help have been identified as those at risk (DWCD 1996).

Alison Phinney puts forward the notion of a trafficking triangle, which refers to the space created by the demand, supply and impunity with which trafficking occurs. According to her, 'sex trafficking is driven by a demand for women's and children's bodies in the sex industry, fuelled by a supply of women denied equal rights and opportunities for education and economic advancement and perpetuated by traffickers who are able to exploit human misfortune with near impunity' (Phinney 2001).

Insufficient or inadequate laws, poor enforcement, ineffective penalties, minimal chances of prosecution, the relatively low risks involved, corruption and complacency, invisibility of the issue, the failure of governments to implement policies and provide adequate services for victims—all play a role in perpetuating trafficking (Warburton 1996; DWCD 1996; Refugee Reports 2000; Phinney 2001; UNDP 2002; Nirmala Niketan, College of Social Work, 2003).

A view that is often not highlighted is that 'people who protest trafficking are in a minority. It is very difficult to fight because everyone is unified—all are involved in trafficking in one way or another. The families are profiting so no one will talk' (HRW 1995). In the context of sexual exploitation of children, a consultation workshop found that the absence of reliable data leads some to emphasise the speculative nature of the problem. This creates a lack of seriousness about the issue, which provides an opportunity for the crime to flourish (DWCD 1996).

Central to the organisation of trafficking are the people who become "highly profitably, low risk, expendable, reusable and resellable commodities" (Richard 1999). This trade in human beings as chattels and treatment of their bodies as commodities becomes possible because of the incremental link between body and money, the end objective of this process always being instrumentalisation for gains. According to Truong (2001) this is a reflection of the 'ongoing, cultural decomposition of the human being through gradual removal of its spirit, personhood, vitality down to bare body parts.'

Notwithstanding the problems of conceptual clarity in the definitions of trafficking, there is broad agreement on the stages involved throughout the literature surveyed. They are listed as recruitment of people from a village or city; transportation to a designated location/transit point; possible shift to a central location; before the move to their ultimate destination. Sometimes the trafficked persons are shifted several times before they arrive at their final destination, where the 'sale' takes place. The different elements involved in this process seem to create an impossible number of permutations and combinations. Thus, most of the research on trafficking resorts to case studies in an attempt to reflect its variations. However, at the regional level, some patterns in these processes can be discerned (ILO 2002a: 14–15).

Place: People are reportedly recruited at places like cinema halls, bus stops, railway stations, airports, streets and their homes. Other places mentioned are cafes, restaurants, beauty contests and beauty parlours. State and national highways, quarry and construction work sites, and areas where locals are displaced without proper rehabilitation may also be sites for potential victims.

Time: Some studies report that traffickers choose special times for recruitment. They take advantage of difficult periods, either before the harvesting season or during a drought, when many locals look elsewhere for income to survive (HRW 1995). Traffickers also keep themselves informed about severely impoverished areas or those which have suffered climatic, economic or political disasters (Johnston and Khan 1998: 53; ISS 2003a). They also reportedly recruit people during festivals (ISS 2003a, and 2003c).

Methods: The range of the tactics or strategies reportedly used vary from the extremely violent (drugging, kidnapping and abduction) to persuasion, material inducements, befriending and deception. People are lured with fake job offers or false marriages. In the South Asian region, offers of marriage without dowries are welcomed; thus, it is easy to arrange fake marriages.

Most studies on prostitution offer some information on the recruitment techniques that are used. (Rozario 1988; ATSEC 2001; SOS 2001; Joshi 2002; ADB 2002: 15). In the CSWB study, 11.90 per cent of the respondents listed deception by someone as a cause for entry into prostitution. The percentages were 23.15 and 27.2 (Mukherjee and Das, 1996: 42). According to another study, 11 per cent of the women were lured, 11 per cent were abducted, and 9.2 per cent were sold and resold (Rozario 1988: 76).

Traffickers approach women and girls in groups as it helps them to win their trust (Sangroula 2001). In India, recent news stories have shown a trend of traffickers using marriage bureaus and placement and tutorial agencies as a front for luring people.

Recruiters/Procurers: Recruiters can be neighbours, friends of families, relatives of friends, acquaintances returned from abroad; women who have migrated or who have been trafficked, women friends returned from abroad; husbands, fathers, boyfriends or lovers. Some recruiters were gay men who were trusted by women because of their sex orientation (Raymond 2002). They can be drug peddlers, head masons at construction sites, even band leaders in dancing/live bars (ISS 2003a), motorcycle pilots as in Goa (CRG 2003) or labour contractors (ISS 2003c). They either use friends and acquaintances to recruit or rely on word of mouth. Terms like *dalal* or *dalali* are used, to refer to traffickers (Nirmala Niketan, College of Social Work, 2003; Gupta 2003).

Characteristics of traffickers: Traffickers are usually young men and middle-aged women who are significantly older than the young women/children they recruit. They are natives and agents who travel back and forth from home countries/regions to receiving regions and generally have links with the villages to which the victims belong. Procurers are reportedly substance abusers or gamblers. Many of the traffickers are older women, who are either former prostitutes or are themselves in forced prostitution, trying to escape abuse and bondage by providing a substitute. Often, these agents speak several languages (Giri 1999: 77, Tumlin 2000). They may have multiple roles. For instance, those who fuel migration, with its outcome in trafficking, may often also be the people who facilitate other, less exploitative, forms of migration, as in the case of refugees (Tumlin 2000). The 'use of words like "mafia" or the depiction of traffickers as villain outsiders do not correspond to the actual garb taken by most traffickers' (Blanchet 2002).

Players: Trafficking is said to involve a range of players 'along the road from acquisition to exploitation' (ILO 2002a: 13). They are generally found in the context of organised trafficking. Networks may involve the police, visa/passport officials, railway/bus authorities and employees, taxi/autorickshaw drivers or rickshaw pullers (DWCD 1996). The various roles have been classified as financiers or investors; procurers or recruiters; organisers; document forgers; corrupt public officials or protectors; brothel operators and the owners and managers of sex establishments; escorts, guides or travel companions and crew members (Richard 1999; Scholenhardt 1999; Raymond 2002). There is also the category of an initial spotter, which is called *choghat/ arkathi* in Bengali (ISS 2003a).

Some additional categories are given by Scholenhardt (1999: 18-20) in the context of smuggling and trafficking, especially cross-border operations. These are informers, enforcers, supporting personnel and specialists, debt-collectors, money-movers and transporters who gather information on matters such as border surveillance, immigration and transit procedures, asylum systems, and law enforcement activities. There are also agents, who pay the recruiter, arrange for travel documents, hold the women until they are ready to leave; and brokers who meet the women on arrival and pay the agent for delivering them.

DWCD (1996) has identified two types of traffickers: primary and secondary. The latter are said to operate behind the scenes with connections in government circles, which are used to provide themselves with protection. Pimps and procurers are the primary traffickers.

Types of operations: People can be trafficked via organised international networks, through local trafficking rings or by occasional traffickers. Thus, traffickers may operate alone, in small gangs or as part of organised crime groups (Richard 1999; Kelly 2001; Icduygu and Toktas 2002). The last two are reportedly the dominant modes of trafficking in South Asia (Government of Sweden 2001; Sanghera 2002; Nirmala Niketan, College of Social Work, 2003). However, a Joint Women's Programme (JWP) study indicates the presence of systematic organised trafficking of girls for profit, for the greatest number of girls brought, transported and sold within and outside India (Shalini and Lalitha 1996: 38). When part of an organised network, traffickers have less freedom and make smaller profits compared to a scenario where they operate on a more independent basis.

Trafficking and organised crime: An organised crime group is defined by the United Nations Convention on Organised Crime as a structured group of three or more, existing for a period of time and 'acting in concert with the aim of committing one or more serious crimes or offences established in accordance with this convention in order to obtain directly or indirectly a financial or other material benefit' (United Nations 2000: 4).

Richard (1999) draws a vivid picture of the involvement of organised crime groups in trafficking in the international context. She notes that in most cases, the operations are sophisticated and global in scale (facilitated by modern technology) with a few exceptions, where trafficking is localised cottage industry. The information that is available on the involvement of organised crime groups, in the literature on trafficking in India, amounts to unsubstantiated references. The involvement is indicated by case studies covered by news reports (Ghosh 1993: 132; Nair 2002: 114). Traffickers operate within zones which are marked and do not usually violate the zone norms. Consequently, when moving from one zone to another, entirely different sets of people take over the activities (ISS 2003a). They also frequently change their area of residence—to not only avoid the police but also to widen their field of operation (*ibid.*)

Trafficking 'patterns and routes are often highly complex, ranging from trafficking within one country and cross-border flows between neighbouring countries to inter-continental and globalised trade' (Tumlin 2000). The general movement of trafficked people is from less developed areas to more developed regions. Thus, the flow of trafficked women and children moves from South to North or East to West, with the former being characterised by poverty and the latter by relative affluence; or from countries in economic, social and political crises to more socially and politically stable countries; or from rural to urban areas. People have been trafficked from South-East Asia and South America to the United Kingdom, Italy, US, etc. They are also being moved towards the Middle East. Some cases of trafficking from India to South-East Asia have been reported. Delhi and Mumbai are said to be the main transit zones for international movement (Haq 2001). Routes are usually divided into origin, transit and destination points; some reports also mention collection and dispersal points. Correspondingly, countries are categorised as sending, transit or destination countries. They may belong to more than one category as in the case of India, which is destination as well as a source, a transit point. Studies identify routes and districts and discuss the problems faced in finding effective solutions to cross-border trafficking. In the Indian context, Nepal and Bangladesh are the two main suppliers. There have been news reports that after the disintegration of USSR, girls from Russia and other CIS countries, like Uzbekistan, were trafficked into India.[3]

Bangladesh: Bangladesh shares a 4,156 km border with 30 districts on the Indian side. India has 20 official checkpoints manned by the Border Security Force (BSF). Being few and widely dispersed, they are ineffective in maintaining strict vigilance over movements across the border. Crossing the border between Bangladesh and West Bengal is a daily routine for many. Thus, keeping track of the movement of people is very difficult. Illegal entries by traffickers are a matter of common knowledge, and there is a perception that they are protected. A number of businesses have developed to facilitate these cross-border movements; each trip may cost no more than Rs. 50 per person (ADB 2002: 16,23). A well-organised bribe system also helps people to cross over the flat terrain (BNWLA 1998). Further, a multiple passports system 'facilitates easy entry of Bangladeshi girls into Kolkata brothels and a close nexus exists between traffickers and border village communities (DWCD 1996).

Once the women enter India, they are kept in West Bengal and Orissa. After being 'sorted and graded', they may be sold to pimps or sent to the Middle East, Kolkata, Bashirghat, Delhi, Mumbai or Agra. Studies conducted by ADB (2002), BNWLA (1998) and Shamim (2001) list detailed trafficking routes in this area.

Nepal: The Indo-Nepal border is a long and porous one with 14 legal entry points along the entire stretch (ADB 2002: 24), which facilitate illegal cross-border movements. 'Under the 1950 Treaty with India, citizens of each country are guaranteed equal treatment, including the same privileges in the matter of residence, participation in trade and commerce. This means in practice that there is no immigration control for Nepalese travelling or migrating to India, and hence no records are maintained' (*ibid.*:18). The ADB study on Nepal lists the districts through which this movement takes place and identifies the entry and exit points as well as the major border regions used by traffickers between Nepal and India.

Internal: Trafficking from neighbouring countries accounts for only 10 per cent of the coerced migration, with approximately 2.17 per cent from Bangladesh and 2.6 per cent from Nepal. The share of interstate trafficking is estimated to be around 89 per cent (ADB 2002: 8). Studies by Rozario (1988), Gathia (1999), Mukherjee (1997), CSWB (1991), SAP (2001) and Haq (2000) provide details of the internal trafficking routes in India, where centres of commercial sexual exploitation are located and the interstate flesh trade triangles. These studies also identify geographical belts of exploitation; for instance, the pink triangle between Agra, Jaipur and Delhi.

Andhra Pradesh, Bihar, Karnataka, Madhya Pradesh, Rajasthan, West Bengal, Uttar Pradesh and Maharashtra appear to be the main states from where trafficked persons are sourced. The metro cities are the most frequent destination points. Rozario et al. (1988) also trace various sellers and market centres. Interstate movement for prostitution was found to be high between Mumbai and Karnataka. Women from Karnataka constitute 45.6 per cent of the prostitutes in Mumbai. Interstate movement in case of women in Bangalore was as high as 72.11 per cent, and 93.60 per cent of the prostitutes in Hyderabad were from within Andhra Pradesh (Mukherjee and Das, 1996: 34-35).

Once they are brought to their destinations, the women may be 'sold' or 'transferred'. Rozario et al. (1988) have identified the market areas in various states and describe the characteristics of the girls being 'sold'. In some places, they are 'resold'. The 'rates' for women range from Rs. 400 to Rs. 70,000 based on criteria such as looks, age, etc. (*ibid.*: 83).

Mechanisms of control: The aim of trafficking is to transfer a person to another place for purposes of exploitation. Thus, various control mechanisms are used to ensure compliance with the exploiters' demands. Trafficked persons may be subjected to three forms of control: physical confinement; monetary control; and all kinds of violence and threats. In fact, violence is an integral part of this process and is used as a means of initiation, intimidation, punishment and control. It 'is the tool by which slavery is achieved, the aim of slavery is profit' (Bales 1999: 246). Thus, situations and circumstances are created where trafficked people have little or no control over their bodies and lives.

Rozario reports up to 18 forms of violence faced by women trafficked for prostitution. They may be starved, locked up in a dark room, beaten, burnt with cigarette butts, bound, forced to drink, strangled, stabbed or killed or not trading their bodies. The women face threats of torture and physical abuse (even their families are not spared), and they may be murdered if they do not cooperate. Attempts are made to create dependency on drugs and alcohol among the victims. Most 'children relent within 7 to 10 days under psychological pressure' and the other tactics used by their exploiters (Nirmala Niketan, College of Social Work, 2003).

The women are often in debt bondage because money is withheld as payback for the purchase price. Bales (1999: 18) refers to this as 'contract' slavery and it is considered extremely profitable. They have little money for sustenance and most report living off tips received. This leads to dependence on traffickers for money, food, clothes and other necessities. The resulting emotional and physical manipulation ensures that the traffickers' activities are kept secret and allows them to maintain control over the victim. Rescued trafficked women fear reprisals by traffickers to whom they are indebted (Raymond 2002; Rozario 1988; Karmakar 2001; Mukherjee 1997; Richard 1999).

Bonded labour: Extraction of labour on the basis of debt bondage is widely prevalent in the sectors served by trafficking. This is especially true of India.[4] In his work on slavery, Bales (1999: 8-9) estimates that the number of slaves in the world is around 27 million, of which 15 to 20 million constitute bonded labour in India, Pakistan, Nepal and Bangladesh. Bonded labour is said to be prevalent in over 20 states of India. Migrant workers have been found to be working under conditions similar to the bonded labour system in fish processing units of Gujarat, stone quarries of Haryana and brick kilns of Punjab (ILO 2001c).

According to Human Rights Watch, at least 15 million children are working as virtual slaves (HRW 1996). Agriculture accounts for 52 to 87 per cent of the population of bonded child labourers. They can also be in bondage working as domestic help; in the domestic, export industries (silk and silk saris, beedi, silver jewellry, synthetic and precious gemstones, footwear and sporting goods, and handwoven wool carpets); and in services like small restaurants, truck stops and tea shops. Other instances of children in forced labour are found in prostitution, begging, drug selling and petty crime. Trafficking of children is specifically reported from the carpet industry (HRW 1996; HRW 2003: 6).

The demand for trafficked persons comes from various sectors. The broad divisions given below have been borrowed from the Haq study on child trafficking.

Trafficking for purposes of commercial sexual exploitation has been widely reported and studied. The relationship between these two processes is a matter of some major confusion and contention, resulting in diverse perspectives and opinions. The different forms that commercial sexual exploitation takes are prostitution, pornography, cybersex and sex tourism.

Prostitution: Prostitution is mainly an economic phenomenon that is grounded in deeply patriarchal values. It involves moral, religious, health and human rights issues. The sector is characterised by economic exploitation, corruption, links with crime and is one which governments find difficult to deal with (Lim 1998). The 'large-scale accumulation of capital takes place through a progressive appropriation and decimation of women's and children's bodies, sexuality and entire beings' (Raymond et al. 2002). The majority of the victims are women and young children, mainly girls.

In India, the most quoted figures to depict the magnitude of prostitution are from the CSWB survey of six metropolitan cities conducted in 1990. According to the study, the total population of prostitutes in all the cities put together is between 70,000 and

100,000 (Mukherjee and Das, 1996). Another report estimates the number of prostitutes to be 900,000 (Gathia 1999). According to the 1992 estimates of the Indian Association for the Rescue of Fallen Women, there are 8 million brothel workers in India and another 7.5 million call girls.

In 1996, the UN Special Rapporteur on Sale of Children, Child Prostitution and Child Pornography stated that 'all reports indicate a dramatic escalation of the number of sexually exploited children all over the world' (Baker 1999). Children are preferred as they are more likely to go along with practices which older prostitutes may refuse. Then there are myths relating to them that feed this preference. For instance, it is believed that sexually transmitted diseases, including HIV infection, can be cured and virility can be increased by having sex with younger girls. Younger girls are also preferred because they can put in more years of work as prostitutes, with high economic gains to be generated from their exploitation (Nirmala Niketan, College of Social Work 2003). These assertions and beliefs are repeated in almost every report on prostitution.

Different organisational structures and hierarchies, modes of operation, and types of prostitutes are described in the available literature (Mukherjee and Das, 1996; Mukherjee 1997; DWCD 1998; ADB 2002). Prostitution is carried out from rooms, apartments, small hotels, exclusive clubs[5], under the guise of call centres, friendship clubs, and beauty and massage parlours; along national highways. A new category that seems to be emerging is that of 'flying prostitutes'. Based on rough estimates, a workshop report concluded that in Delhi "the number of prostitutes operating outside the purview of regular brothel system would be several times more, since GB Road accommodates only about 3,000 prostitutes and police sources state that there are 'around 10,000 to 15,000 female prostitutes in Delhi' (Gupta 2003). Thus, commercial sexual exploitation takes place at various locations, which keep shifting. The working conditions may depend on the type of establishment.

Other players in the sector are pimps who are considered to be the 'pillars of the sex industry, viewed as protectors and more welcome than police' (DWCD 1996). Clients are profiled as men separated from their families, visitors in tourist and religious centres other abusers, businessmen, politicians, transport operators, drivers, cleaners, migrant labourers, students and tourists (Shalini and Lalitha 1996). The nexus between prostitution, politicians and government officials is frequently revealed by press reports.[6]

The degree of financial independence they enjoy varies among prostitutes (Karmakar 2001; Shalini and Lalitha 1996; Mukherjee and Das, 1996). Regarding overall profits, Kamathipura (in Mumbai) alone generates at least US $400 million per year, with 100,000 prostitutes servicing men 365 days per year, averaging 6 customers per day, at $2 per customer. Another study estimated that transactions in prostitution were worth Rs. 185,000,000 in a day and Rs. 37,000 crores per year (Gathia 1999: 20). Children as young as nine years of age are purchased for Rs. 60,000 at auctions where Arab bid against Indian men (SOS 2001). Quoting from various studies, classifies prostitutes according to the degree of control they have over the money they earn. Around 117 were totally dependent, 158 were practically dependent and 65 were independent. A study on GB Road in Delhi found that 15.4 per cent of the prostitutes had no idea of their earnings, as controlling agents cornered all their earnings (Shalini and Lalitha 1996). The sharing of income forms an integral part of the sex business. This 'sharing of income makes the nexus between procurers, pimps, brothel keepers, local goondas and police so strong that they together promote prostitution' (Mukherjee and Das, 1996: 67).

Two main patterns of trafficking for commercial sexual exploitation have been documented. The 'traditional "two-step" pattern targets women already working in prostitution to be trafficked abroad, whereas the more aggressive "one-step" pattern targets women and young girls directly in their villages to be trafficked for prostitution abroad. With the increased demand for younger women arising from the fear of HIV infection, the "one-step" pattern is beginning to dominate' (United Nations 2000).

Unique to India are the traditions of devadasis and jogins. Some communities induct their daughters into prostitution, and the boys start pimping for family members at the age of 15. These well-documented recruitment practices have an element of coercion (Gathia 1999; DWCD 1998; Giri 1999; IDS 2003; SAKHI 2003; ISS 2003c).

Usually women and girls belonging to the most disadvantaged sections of society are found in prostitution. Nearly 50 per cent are from Scheduled Castes and Scheduled Tribes and 12 to 27 per cent from Other Backward Classes (DWCD 1998). Recent press reports indicate a trend of girls from affluent backgrounds being lured into the sex trade; married women too enter the trade for short periods (two months), with the consent of their husbands.[7] The plight of children of prostitutes is reported to be dismal (Nirmala Niketan, College of Social Work 2003).

Sex tourism: The growth of the tourism industry has contributed to the increase in the sexual exploitation of children, which often assumes intolerable forms. Sex tourism, or tourism for purposes of sex, has found its way into the mainstream tourism market (DWCD 1998; CRG 2003). Tourism creates conditions which facilitate an easy indulgence. The benefit of anonymity offered by the host country reduces the element of the external inhibitory factors to the minimum. South Asian countries are preferred because of the lax law enforcement. Sex tourism involves travel agencies, tour operators, hotels and others in the tourism industry; some companies even openly 'adverstise availability of child prostitutes' (Nirmala Niketan, College of Social Work, 2003). Paedophiles are said to be the dominant 'clientele' in sex tourism (Desai 2001: 38, 41; NCW 1997).

A recent study found that children who had 'direct interaction with customers features high on the list of children who were sexually exploited by tourists'. The commercial sexual exploitation of children 'differs based on the type of tourism that exists' (Equations 2002: 46). Sex tourism is reportedly prevalent in the states of Rajasthan, Goa (a major destination) and Kerala in India, while Mumbai is believed to be the 'biggest centre for paedophiliac commerce in India' (Nirmala Niketan, College of Social Work 2003). A study on tourism-related commercial sexual exploitation of children on the eastern coast of India found that out of a sample of 150 children, 60 per cent had come to the tourist area on being promised a better job, accompanied by a 'neighbourhood uncle'. It also found that 40 per cent of the children interviewed mentioned 'force' as the means used for instance, moneylenders forcing parents to sell their children to repay debts (Equations 2002: 33). Another reports states that 'hotels have contacts with adult sex workers, pimps and other middlemen – rikshaw pullers, van pullers, petty traders. These people make contact with street children and bring them to tourist lodges and hotels as per the demand placed by customers' (Equations 2003:28)

The problem of labour exploitation is widely prevalent in India. According to the Supreme Court definition, all those who are paid less than the stipulated minimum wages fall within the category of bonded labourers. At present there are 35 crore workers in the unorganised sector who are not paid the prescribed minimum wages. Besides there are 12 crore children of the age 6 to 14 who are not going to schools. Thus 47 crore people a little less than half of the population of India are in the state of bondage' (Iyer 2003: 436). Estimates of the number of child labourers in India vary from 60 million to 115 million.

Trafficking for purposes of labour exploitation has not been sufficiently researched. Among the few studies conducted, an important one by ILO on trafficking in Nepal, and sexual abuse among street children in Kathmandu, found that all the 14 victims were trafficked either for purposes of domestic child labour, or to work as hotel boys or as labour in the carpet weaving industry (Subedi 2002: iii). Children trafficked for labour exploitation may also be subjected to sexual abuse and exploitation. Employers prefer to hire children because they cost less, are easier to cheat, exploit and intimidate, and are hard-working (Nirmala Niketan, College of Social Work, 2003; ISS 2003b).

Besides being forced to work as domestic labour or being exploited by the small-scale sector, people are trafficked for agricultural, construction or industrial work (organised and unorganised). They may be trafficked for performing illegal activities—like drug peddling, organ trading, forced marriages, begging—or be sold off by adoption rackets. Trafficking for entertainment and sports, like camel racing, for exotic dancing or the circus is also reported.

The impact of the experience of trafficking on the physical and mental health of the victims has not been properly documented and analysed (Government of Sweden 2001). Reports about the consequences vary, depending on whether the end purpose is included in the adopted definition of trafficking. Thus, some studies may include instances of human rights violation that occur at the destinations; others may not. Trafficking has health, social, legal and economic effects on the victims (Wennerholm 2002).

Trafficked persons are reportedly traumatised by their experiences. Depression and suicidal thoughts are commonly reported. The mental and emotional state of the survivors may include malevolence, helplessness and withdrawal; disassociation; self-blame and identification with the aggressor; distraction; a foreshortened view of time; normalisation and shaping, whereby the victims convince themselves that their experiences had to happen instead of viewing them as traumatic (Saarthak 2002: 3-6). Some of the psychiatric disorders among survivors of trafficking are listed as posttraumatic stress disorder, depressive disorder, dissociative disorders, psychotic disorders and eating disorders (*ibid.*: 7). Girls are made to bear the responsibility of upholding the family honour through their sexual purity/chastity (ISS 2003c). If they are trafficked into CSE (commercial sexual exploitation), they face additional stress because of the prevalent morality.

Besides being stigmatised as outcasts and facing moral and legal isolation (Giri 1999: 68), trafficked people are vulnerable to HIV/AIDS infection[8], drug addiction; and high-risk abortions and teenage pregnancies, which may affect their reproductive health for life. A study by an NGO in Dhaka found that 'more than 20 per cent of street children prostitutes die before reaching adulthood.... Almost 22 per cent become physically invalid and are fit only for begging' (SOS 2001: 22). Psychological trauma permeates all aspects of their lives. Since it usually remains unaddressed and unresolved, 'the abused turn into abusers' (*ibid.*), with a high probability of them becoming criminals. The consequences of being in 'child labour' and its adverse impact on the development of children are well documented.

The victims of trafficking are compelled to lead illegal lives.

Illegality taints every dimension of their lives, converting into criminals. Their criminalisation as workers and persons severely stigmatizes them. It intensifies their victimization several folds and leaves them with no recourse for redress (Sanghera 2002: 8–9).

There is also a viewpoint which is generally not expressed in the literature on trafficking. It argues that there are conflicting aspects to the social impacts of trafficking, as for many women, trafficking episodes, while causing harm, also removed them from otherwise oppressive circumstances. Thousands of women, who have returned, but remain silent about their experiences, especially concerning CSW, may have brought back not only some savings, but also more experience of the world. Some of these women have managed to turn these experiences into personal empowerment within their communities (ADB 2002: 46).

The crime of trafficking involves the violation of a whole gamut of laws and human rights. It becomes a threat to society because traffickers operate across borders with impunity, with the growing involvement of organised criminals and by generally undermining the rule of law. Trafficking 'threatens the very fabric of society' because it involves not only criminals but also law enforcers. It manifests and perpetuates patriarchal attitudes and behaviour, which undermine the efforts to promote gender equality and eradicate discrimination against women and children (ADB 2002: 45). This is illustrated by reports from Albania, which 'document villages where nine in 10 girls over 14 stay away from school because they are afraid of being trafficked'. Thus, this fear 'alters the choices that girls make about their futures' (ILO 2002a: 29). Similar instances have been reported in the survey by BNWLA.

A study by Asian Development Bank notes that the 'economic losses to communities and governments are enormous if considered in terms of lost returns on human or social capital investments. The cost of countering criminal trafficking activities puts additional strain on the already limited government resources for law enforcement. A vast amount of potential income from trafficked labour is lost in 'hidden' sectors' (ADB 2002: 46). Specific communities may become known as potential sources for people if following each other's example, communities start a trend of sending their children and women out.

The loss of future productivity and earning power through low educational levels, ill health and potentially premature death is also felt at the country and regional level. Poor nations can ill afford to lose their young people, whose present and future productive capacity is essential to growth.... The ravage of disease, including HIV/AIDS, is also an enormous burden on such countries and causes further imbalances between the young and middle-aged potential workforce (most likely to be affected) and older people dependent on them (ILO 2002a: 29).

There is almost no accurate data available on cross-border flows because of the complexities in regulations, which vary from country to country. There is no law on repatriation, no NCRB category under which it is documented and no government enforcement agency which has been able to collect verifiable data. Only NGOs working in the field are able to provide data on this aspect (ADB 2002: 22). The combined estimates for Nepal and Bangladesh range from 500 a year (*ibid.*: 24) to around 7,000 a year (SOS 2001: 25) to 10,000 girls (UNDP 2002: 8) to 5,000 and 7,000 girls being annually trafficked (Tumlin 2000) to more than 200,000 over a period of seven years (SOS 2001: 15). A study by UNDP (2002: 8) shows that the average age of trafficked girls from Nepal to India fell from 14–16 years in the 1980s to 10–14 years in 1994.

The Asian Development Bank report also quotes a data on the number of women trafficked in to Indian brothels collected by various sources. For instance, of the 1,000 to 10,000 women found in Kolkata brothels, 70 per cent are from Bangladesh as reported by Sanlaap (ADB 2002: 21). There are 100,000 to 160,000 Nepali girls in Indian brothels, with about 5,000 to 7,000 being sold every year (Joshi 2002). Other estimates put the figure at 200,000 Nepalese women in Indian brothels (ADB 2002: 21). According to Reuters, 30,000 women in Kolkata brothels are from Bangladesh and another 10,000 are in Mumbai and Goa. The percentage of trafficked Bangladeshi women is 13.5 in Kolkata, 0.2 in Mumbai and 2.6 in Delhi (Joshi 2002). A study of bar girls in Mumbai found that 42 per cent were from Bangladesh (SOS 2001).

The ADB study also cites data on rescue and repatriation operations. As per STOP figures, 70 child victims were repatriated to Nepal during August-February 2002. According to Sanlaap, 65 women were rescued and repatriated from Delhi to Bangladesh in 2001 (ADB 2002: 27-28).

Almost all the studies quote the United Nations figures, which estimate trafficking to be a US $5- 7 billion operation annually. Richard (1999) points out that profits from trafficking are a major source of income for crime rings. To increase profits, inflated prices for various services and documents are charged in cases of cross-border trafficking. The women are kept in poor, crowded conditions to cut down costs. Some Thai traffickers who incarcerated Thai women and men in sweatshops are estimated to have made $8 million over six years (Richard 2001). Indian estimates of revenues from trafficking are not available; usually only figures for selling and purchasing girls are mentioned. According to one estimate, girls are sold to brothels for Rs. 15,000-40,000 (HRW 1995: 2). Commercial sexual exploitation of children 'accounts for Rs. 11000 crores of the Rs. 40,000 crore commercial sex industry' in India (Gupta 2003).

The relative lack of information and quantitative data on trafficking stems from various dimensions of the problem, which make accurate assessments difficult. The clientele wish to remain anonymous, the clandestine nature of the traffickers' activities, the low visibility of exploitation itself, and the victims fear of the police and their exploiters—all ensure that few details are revealed. Thus, researchers find it difficult to locate sources and face-non-cooperation from most of the entities involved (Phinney 2001: 3; Blanchet 2002; Pandey, Jena and Mohanty, 2002; DWCD 1998). This probably explains why a majority of the studies have very small sample sizes. Their emphasis on qualitative rather than quantitative data limits the emergence of patterns and trends. To date, the only study to be conducted on trafficking at an all-India level based on field research is by Rozario (1988). Many reports use news stories, law enforcement agencies and antitrafficking programmes as their sources of information, which influence the conclusions they arrive at. As Blanchet observes, 'studies on the trafficking in women carried out from such establishments (rehabilitation homes) do not adequately represent the life path of most "trafficked" women'. The complexity of the cases makes it difficult to apply standard definitions to specific instances. Trafficking 'stories are difficult to squeeze in [to] little boxes' (Blanchet 2002). In the context of slavery, Bales notes that 'people are inventive and flexible, and the permutations of human violence and exploitation are infinite' (1999:19). This is equally applicable to the concept of trafficking.

The multi-faceted nature of trafficking is also reflected in the different approaches, that have been adopted to understand and combat trafficking. They represent the intersection points between trafficking and other phenomenon, occurring at various junctures of the trafficking process. Most of the approaches have overlapping elements. For instance, an approach will generally bring a gender or labour perspective to the problem. At the same time, the problem will be also be discussed within the framework of human rights. This is the most inclusive, covering the maximum range of issues raised by trafficking.

Adopted approaches and perspectives influence the strategies that are designed for combating trafficking. Sanghera (1997: 27) states that in South Asia, trafficking is addressed as a problem of crime and violence against women, exploitation of children and child labour, or within a sociological framework. Only recently attempts have begun to view it from a human rights perspective'. Trafficking may be approached as an issue of labour, crime, migration, human rights, development, children's rights or gender (Derks 2000; Wijers 2002).

When approached as a moral or a prostitution issues in India, two distinct camps exist. One supports legalisation of prostitution as a profession through self-regulatory boards constituted by sex workers, which will check the inflow of new entrants, especially with respect to age and health. The anti-legislation lobby believes that legalisation will merely legitimise an exploitative sector and strengthen the position of brothel owners and pimps. Moreover, guardians will justify their acts by pointing out that their wards have joined a legitimate profession (Shalini and Lalitha 1996).

There have been recent attempts at unionisation among women in prostitution. The Mahila Samanwaya Committee in Calcutta came together in a national conference of sex workers in 1997.

However, the JWP study by Shalini and Lalitha found that organisations have underlying political and vested interests in the formation of such groups. Barring the demands for crèche services and education of their women, the other demands are a betrayal of the interests of women.

The broad areas of intervention in trafficking have been laid down in the UN protocol as prevention, protection and assistance. The report of the United Nations High Commissioner goes on to recommend principles and guidelines under these very broad divisions (UNESCAP 2002). Most reports on trafficking devote more than half the space to interventions and recommendations. The two broad areas under which these are covered are the criminal justice system and social welfare policies (United Nations 2001). The former includes nationals laws and international instruments that are relevant to trafficking. Usually, the role of the implementation agencies and the policies and programmes of the government and non-government agencies are discussed. Two studies sponsored by the UNICEF, which are presently underway, have as their main objectives, the assessment of rescue and rehabilitation measures and facilities. One of them is an all-India study, which looks at government rehabilitation institutions for trafficked people in all the 35 states and UTs.

The 'four primary reasons for inappropriate or inadequate responses' to trafficking are denial of the problem; objectifying the victims and failing to consider their human rights; conflation of trafficking with undocumented migration; and an improper definition of the crime (Jordon 2002).

In her critique of the trafficking laws in South Asia, Sanghera (1999) argues that the legal system is disempowering trafficked persons through an erosion of their constitutional and human rights in an ostensible attempt to protect them from harm and abuse—an impact that is contrary to aims of anti-trafficking measures. She also points out that the laws do not address cases of women rescued as adults but those who may have been trafficked as children, thereby infantilising women (Sanghera 1999).

Judiciary: Two widely mentioned Supreme Court judgements – *Vishal Jeet v. Union of India in 1990* and *Gaurav Jain v. Union of India in 1997* – are considered instrumental in initiating government action on the issue of commercial sexual exploitation (DWCD 1998).

On the other hand, the judiciary is accused of playing a role in secondary victimization through its mode of questioning during court procedures and the long and tedious processes involved. The legal system is perceived to be formidable by the victims rather than being a deterrent to those who commit offences (DWCD 1996). Depending on the sensitivity of the judges, judgements, range from supporting the victims to aggravating their harassment (United Nations 2001).

Generally, Indian courts send rescued girls who are foreign nationals, for example Nepalese or Bangladeshis, back to their countries with the help of NGOs; sometimes, they are sent to government homes. Beyond that, there is hardly any activism or inquiry. 'Very little action is taken by the police or the judiciary against the traffickers and those who are initially responsible for the violation of the rights of these women.... With regard to the evidentiary procedures involved in trafficking cases, the women and girls who are victims of the trafficking are the primary witnesses against the perpetrators. In cases involving organised crime, they are extremely vulnerable and in fear for their lives' (United Nations 2001: 16).

Police: In the SAARC region, the police forces of the respective countries meant to be are 'the most important institutions in the struggle to eradicate trafficking' (United Nations 2001: 15). In reality though, police involvement in trafficking is indicated in all the reports and corruption within the force is said to be 'endemic' (*ibid.*).

In the literature surveyed, the police are accused of supporting brothel owners, being in complicity with traffickers and according the crime of trafficking a low priority (HRW 1995; DWCD 1996; DWCD 1998; United Nations 2001). The conduct and management of rescue operations has been severely criticised. Reports are critical about the behaviour of police personnel, age verification procedures and the lack of appropriate networking with other concerned agencies; for instance, protective homes (STOP 2002a: 26; ADB 2002b: 32; Nirmala Niketan, College of Social Work 2003).

Prostitutes prefer to be under the protection of a brothel owner, as the latter negotiate with policemen who are seen as tormentors and are looked upon with hatred in the sex industry (DWCD 1996). STOP (2002a) elaborates on some very detailed deficiencies in the investigations, which results in the acquittal of the accused. Legislation requires the police force to play a more proactive role, as they have been given preventive responsibility. However, they usually limit their involvement to taking reactive measures and addressing the manifestations of the crime, rather than its roots (DWCD 1996).

The problems faced by police personnel have also been highlighted. They fear levelling of allegations and victimisation by brothel owners who use their political links. The police experience difficulties in sending children to juvenile homes due to poor facilities and in communicating with them. Understaffing, especially in rural areas, does not allow them to devote sufficient attention to trafficking in terms of surveillance and prevention. Victims generally turn hostile (DWCD 1996). The lack of infrastructure and resources; and the powerful political and business connections of trafficking are also mentioned as inhibiting the law enforcement machinery (DWCD 1998). Rapid prosecution is also hindered by the lack of any authority to investigate a crime beyond the state level; the CBI is said to face many challenges. The working and living conditions of the constabulary are reported to be dismal (ADB 2002: 63). There is 'lack of per capita time for the constable or sub inspector at the grassroots (i.e. police constable per thousand is low) due to other law/order priorities' (*ibid.*).

Other factors: Trafficked people also come into contact with immigration officials and border forces. Some reportedly collaborate with the traffickers. Many trafficked women allege that immigration officials are involved in the process of their transfer because of a noticeable lack of questioning and examination of their documents (Raymond et al. 2002). They may support trafficking by selling visas (GSN 1997).)

The literature from other regions is concerned with the use of new technologies in trafficking, which is generally not expressed in Indian literature. From the point of view of prosecution, 'developments in methods of detection and prevention have not kept pace with the creation of new forms of trafficking' (Giri 1999: 72). A few studies do indicate that trafficking may call for more sophisticated and innovative investigation techniques because of the use of these communication tools and the role of organised crime involving international syndicates (ADB 2002: 63; Nair 2002).

The main government body dealing with protection and assistance policies and programmes is the Department of Women and Child Development (DWCD) under the Ministry of Human Resource Development. It is the national focal point for combating trafficking in women and children in India. DWCD has corresponding departments in each state government (ADB 2002: 48). The 1990 Supreme Court judgement in the *Vishal Jeet v. Union of India* case directed the government to ensure care, protection, development, treatment and rehabilitation of the victims of commercial sexual exploitation and the setting up of a central advisory committee. It was constituted in the same year and a national seminar was also held. The Central Social Welfare Board initiated a survey, which led to a national consultation in 1994. This was followed by six regional workshops, organised to formulate strategies involving the various stakeholders (DWCD 1998).

National Plan: In 1998 a national action plan was formulated by DWCD to combat trafficking and the commercial sexual exploitation of women (DWCD 1998a). The plan covered various aspects, such as prevention, awareness raising, economic empowerment, rescue and rehabilitation. Coomarasamy notes that it contained innovative ideas, with the social welfare component being dealt with in detail—from rescue and rehabilitation, to education of the children of prostitutes, to housing and shelter. She commends 'the effort to include psychological counselling as an aspect to health care' and observes that health services have been adequately covered (United Nations 2001: 32).

However, the plan has been criticised for lacking an 'integrated perspective on intelligence relating to trafficking-rescue-rehabilitation-reintegration' (SAP 2001: 54). The other shortcomings are that it lacks details of funding, does not cover child pornography and is likely to run into implementation bottlenecks (*ibid*: 53). The 'suggestion that the children of prostitutes be removed from their mothers to more healthy environments' is a 'disturbing violation of the right to family even if it is done with good intentions' (United Nations 2001: 32). The method of 'social surveillance' to combat trafficking is not considered advisory and the rapporteur comments that 'accountable state institutions are better vehicles for enforcement than social surveillance'. The plan is silent on 'laws and strategies for finding and punishing traffickers' (*ibid*.).

Prevention: The ADB country report on India describes various poverty alleviation and pro-women schemes launched by different ministries that may prevent vulnerable sections from being trafficked. The report acknowledges that effective source area programming calls for a holistic outlook, as adopted by the Working Women's Forum (ADB 2002: 78). Among the government initiatives mentioned are the Integrated Child Development Scheme (ICDS) and Swarn Jayanthi Swarozgar Yojana.

The Swadhar scheme, which was initiated in December 2001, is meant for women in difficult circumstances, including rescued victims of trafficking (Department of Women and Child Development 2001). The DWCD also plans to formulate a national media strategy. State level initiatives are being handled by the state partners. The Jabali scheme in Madhya Pradesh addresses the Bhedia, Bhancadara and Sansi tribes and brings a holistic approach to programmes for the children of victims (*ibid*.: 57).

Rehabilitation: The process of rehabilitation mainly involves sending women to government-run homes for protective custody until their cases are heard or they are sent back to their original homes. These government run homes have been criticised for a host of short comings - corruption, poor infrastructure facilities, meager budgets, inadequate provisions for psychological care, ineffective skill building (DWCD 1996). Most women end up doing nothing for long periods, while those who do not wish to be rescued view the home as a prison. They are confined to the vicinity of the homes. 'Protective custody as practised in South Asia is a serious violation of women's rights and it is important that Governments of the region re-examine this concept, as well as the conditions in the government homes where women are kept' (United Nations 2001: 12).

Apparently, the Bombay High Court has ordered that these homes be supervised by outside authorities (ADB 2002: 61). States like Haryana have failed to provide short-stay homes for minor girls.[9] The lack of appropriate facilities has meant that the rescued girls are forced to stay in nari niketans, which is illegal. Short-stay homes with the help of the DWCD and juvenile homes are supposed to be set up under the Juvenile Justice Act for the protection and rehabilitation of minor girls (Gupta 2003). Though all the required states are to provide such homes, only some have done so. The homes that have been set up are overcrowded and are not sufficiently equipped to address basic primary needs. The Juvenile Welfare Board has also been criticised for functioning in relative isolation (Nirmala Niketan, College of Social Work 2003).

The rehabilitation of victims of trafficking can be a complex business. For instance a minor girl who became pregnant refused to have an abortion after being 'rescued'.[10] In cases where the parents are considered unfit or unreliable, these children need to be institutionalised. However, there are very few poster homes. In the absence of a special court to take up the issue, charge of the child is relinquished to the parents. This is problematic as the child is likely to be retrafficked (Nirmala Niketan, College of Social Work 2003). There have also been cases of victims of CSE having organised themselves, continuously resist against eviction and closure of brothels, and demanding appropriate rehabilitation facilities before any such action is taken.

Reintegration: Social stigma and non-acceptability are said to the greatest obstacles to reintegration (DWCD 1998; United Nations

2001; ADB 2002: 65; Shah 2003). Besides the difficulties in finding alternative employment because of the stigma, any livelihood option which pays less than Rs. 2,000 to 3,000 a month is not viable and the rescued girls often lapse back into commercial sex work (ADB 2002: 65).

Some studies have concluded that there are not enough models of recovery, repatriation and reintegration based on prioritising the preference and interests of trafficked women and children (Sanghera 1999: 24; ADB 2002: 65). There is also a dearth of holistic rehabilitation programme and a lack of support mechanisms.

The media hinders the process of rehabilitation by sensationalising the issue and exposing the identities of the victims.

Patterns of media coverage: 'Media coverage as far as the problem of trafficking of women and children is concerned concentrates on activities related to commercial sexual exploitation of women and children' and not the entire process of trafficking. Media reports focus on 'exploitation of sex workers in the hands of brothel owners, pimps, law enforcement agencies; nexus between politicians, traffickers and enforcement agencies; initiatives taken by NGOs and other civil society organisations; case studies of particular victims; incidents of police raids on brothel houses and arrests of people caught during the raids; and events, seminars, workshops organised on the problem of trafficking' (*ibid.*).

Rescued foreign women: There are no laws in India covering repatriation for trafficked persons to Bangladesh and Nepal. It is carried out by NGOs which 'have built relationships with several NGOs across the border to liase with the Nepal Embassy and Bangladesh High Commission in repatriation of trafficked women and children' (ADB 2002: 26). There are reportedly around 200 women waiting to be repatriated to Bangladesh (*ibid.*: 27). Girls are rescued and left at the borders or languish in hoes and are invariably pushed back into prostitution (DWCD 1998). Besides this, not much information is available on the problems faced in reintegrating Bangladeshi or Nepali women and children. NGOs and partner organisations only facilitate repatriation across the national border of India to Nepal and Bangladesh, not within the country itself.

Other Agencies: The Ministry of Home Affairs of the Government of India (centre–state division), the National Commission for Women, the National Human Rights Commission and National AIDS Control Society are some of the government bodies engaged in activities to combat trafficking. Their initiatives are covered in detail by the literature on trafficking. Over 80 NGOs are working in the area of child trafficking and commercial sexual exploitation. Some of the prominent ones are YMCA, ECPAT, JWP, Sanlaap, Prerna, STOP, Prajwala, CACT and Haq. On the political front, 'national politicians and public health officials seem to be in a state of denial of the seriousness of the problem' (Nirmala Niketan, College of Social Work 2003).

Sanghera has called for greater clarity on the concept of trafficking pointing to the need to broaden it to include other purposes besides prostitution. The absence of reliable data, inadequate advocacy efforts, the lack of analysis of laws, insufficient understanding of the human rights framework, limited interventions for prevention, and the lack of human standards for the treatment of victims are some of the gaps in the anti-trafficking initiatives that she has pointed out (1999: 23–24). Brian (2001: 1) describes trafficking as a crime whose victims have to be rescued and protected. However, anti-trafficking initiatives are usually dressed up as anti-migration programmes, adopting strategies for preventive or safe migration. It has also been observed that 'sex workers and migrants are the groups currently challenging the impact of anti-trafficking measures on their rights, which also testifies to the fact that anti-trafficking measures are not dealing with the problems that they set out to address' (Kapur 2001).

Some of the trends reported in the literature suggest that there is not only a significant rise in trafficking but also an increase in its magnitude. Trafficking is said to be 'acquiring grave dimensions worldwide in the recent context of globalisation' (United Nations: 2000; D'Cunha 2002; US Report 2002). This trend is 'alongside an increase in illegal and undocumented migration within the region' (Sanghera 1999). The flows have widened to include most countries of the globe with new sources and destination sites (*ibid.*; D'Cunha 2002: 3). There is a rise in the 'global sophistication, complexity and consolidation of trafficking networks' which is said to incorporate diverse and sophisticated mechanisms (Richard 1999; Raymond 2002; D'Cunha 2002); there is also a greater penetration by organised crime syndicates (Sanghera 1999; Richard 1999).

While people are trafficked for other purposes commercial sexual exploitation remains the most dominant driver (D'Cunha 2002: 3). Attention has also been drawn to 'its complex socioeconomic and political basis underscored by class, gender and ethnic concerns' (*ibid.*). There is a reported preference for very young children and the inclusion of men (DWCD 1996; Government of Sweden 2001; D'Cunha 2002: 3). Other trends summarised by D'Cunha, and covered by almost all the reports, are 'hefty profits, which according to some estimates exceed that of the underground narcotics and arms trade...strong connections between trafficking networks and public officials...vertical and horizontal linkages between trafficking networks and sectors of the crime industry and corporate enterprise, including transport, tourism' (*ibid.*). It has also been observed that 'in the present context of globalisation and migration, fewer victims are being kidnapped or abducted. In fact, an overwhelming majority are being trafficked through deception and false promises' (United Nations 2001; Sanghera 1999).

The literature on trafficking reflects the dilemma of writing on a subject that is not easy to research and document and yet is too grave an issue to ignore. Considering the hidden and criminal nature of the problem, the data presented by most reports is valuable in face of this scarcity. While the adopted definitions, perspectives and approaches to the problem of trafficking may vary the concern with finding effective solutions is common to these studies. The content and format of the majority of the studies are repetitive and appear to be recycled; so much so that the reports are indistinguishable from one another. Their objectives appear to be establishing the occurrence of trafficking, reporting the lacunae in the responses by different agencies and making recommendations. The information on trafficking is presented in a narrative form or is a recording of incidents, events and cases. Much of the literature on trafficking reflects a high degree of outrage.

Most of the reports are on trafficking for commercial sexual exploitation, which is a reflection of the general understanding, till recently, of the association between trafficking and commercial sexual exploitation. The issues in the literature on trafficking echo the debates and concerns about commercial sexual exploitation. Thus, one finds that a seemingly new idea being pursued is invariably an offshoot of the fundamental debate about consent in commercial sexual exploitation.

Generally, the studies focus on children and some even club women and children together. Those focusing on women are few in numbers, and any including men are non-existent.

So far, there have been no studies which have dealt exclusively with the issue of trafficking for labour exploitation. This is understandable given the recent inclusion of this purpose in the definition of trafficking. Numerous studies on child labour and labour exploitation fail to focus on the recruitment practices of the problem. They merely mention that there is exploitation by dalals and children work for agents. These studies consistently report cases that fall within the purview of trafficking. However, since the concept seems to be unfamiliar or unclear, these cases are grouped under the broader notion of exploitation.

According to Sanghera, the discourse on trafficking in South Asia is dominated by 15 myths. The reason they are myths is that none of the assumptions made is founded on any evidence-based data or research. She states that there is an 'urgent need to develop and fine tune methodological aspects such as theoretical constructs, methodological principles, research techniques and tools, and methods for collecting data on trafficking' (Sanghera 1999: 27).

One of the major gaps is the lack of studies on trafficking in India based on primary data. The data collected over the past decades is woefully inadequate. There has been no systematic attempt to gather information in an innovative manner at any significant level. Much of the data that is based on news reports differs only in the incidence reported from various regions.

The information available is in bits and pieces, thereby reducing its value and undermining the efforts to combat trafficking. There is a need to organise, collate and analyse the available information and knowledge. Even with the available database, an analysis of the various dimensions of trafficking is possible, but most studies fail to do so. In the absence of an in-depth analysis of the issues and aspects involved, they have failed to arrive an realistic picture of the scope of the trafficking problem, what sustains it, and why it occurs. The varied dimensions and aspects of trafficking and their interrelationships need to be examined at length instead of being accorded superficial treatment, be it trafficking and migration or trafficking and organised crime.

An important question that needs to be addressed is, why among people in similar positions of vulnerability only some get trafficked while others don't? There is not enough data on how traffickers select their targets. While exploring vulnerability, the role of influential people in a victim's life has not been looked at. The involvement of local communities needs to be studied. To what extent does poor awareness render people vulnerable to the traffickers' designs requires to be explored.

Adequate information on the involvement of organised crime is not available; it is merely hinted at. Nor is there enough knowledge about traffickers, their networks and organisations. There is insufficient clarity about the role of various players in trafficking networks. The characteristics of traffickers, including their socio-economic profiles, have not been thoroughly studied. Nor has the organised nature of trafficking, where the power equations are against the victim, been dealt with. Sanghera (1999: 27) has urged that methodological guidelines to be developed on how to study an underground phenomenon and to fill the gaps in the data on traffickers and organized crime syndicates.

The demand (patterns and trends) side of trafficking has not been adequately examined, and hardly any attempts have been made to understand it. Another important question that needs to be answered is whether 'the demand side of the equation is driven by customer interest or merely that trafficked women are more profitable for sex industry entrepreneurs' or are both factors operating simultaneously, 'serving a mutual interest between suppliers and customers' (Kelly 2002: 33). Maybe the perspectives of the 'clientele' need to be studied.

While there are reference to the nexus between politicians and the police force in media reports, there are no studies to corroborate these stories.

Information on the government and NGOs responses to trafficking, and the measures taken, including preventive steps to combat it, is scanty; for instance data on anti-trafficking networks and their activities. The judgements of various courts that have relevance to trafficking have not been looked at. Nor have the counter-trafficking initiatives been critically analysed in terms of their impact—whether and to what extent do the programmes address the felt needs of the potential victims. The long-term records of women who have been reintegrated are not available. Not much is known about retrafficking. There is a lack of clarity on the issues dealt with in respect of interstate and international trafficking. Interception is another area that has not been sufficiently covered. Studies raise the question of rescue but not of recovering trafficked persons in transit. The circumstances that compel women to enter commercial sexual exploitation are different, and rehabilitation measures need to be sensitive to these variations. This awareness is not reflected in the studies on commercial sexual exploitation and the official responses to the problem.

The existing literature on trafficking does not discuss the complexities of the issue. For instance, if people are trafficked for various purposes and separate laws already exist to address these different forms of exploitation, then does combating trafficking require a special law that will cover all the dimensions of the problem. Examining this question will also help clarify the concept of trafficking, as it brings to fore its intersections with other forms of exploitation. Trafficked persons should be rescued at the sites of exploitation and various provisions may already exist for their rehabilitation. However, these may not be sensitive to the specific problems that trafficked people face in addition to the exploitative purpose for which they have been trafficked.

There is an absence of the understanding that the purpose of trafficking is to put people in slave-like conditions or conditions of forced labour. This could be in various sectors, be it begging or domestic work. Thus, the literature on trafficking manages to establish its occurrence and the steps involved. But it lacks an in-depth analysis of the problem in all its dimensions and the responses of various agencies.

Being a complex phenomenon, trafficking can be viewed from different perspectives. Thus, it is important to acknowledge the standpoint from which it is being approached from. The problem is deeply rooted in the socio-economic, political and cultural reality of the context in which it occurs, although this may not be its immediate cause. The culprits are the traffickers about whom relatively little is known. This gap has to be urgently addressed, along with the demand factors which drive trafficking. It is a fundamental violation of the rights of human beings and shows a blatant disregard for the dignity of a person.

Trafficking is a phenomenon shrouded in ambiguities involving issues which most would prefer to avoid. As suggested by a UNDP study, it is a subject wrapped in layers of silence. The process of clarity will involve numerous debates and arguments. This search is an indicators of the attempts, some successful, of various agencies to bring this issue on the agenda of governments and other concerned authorities. One may say that it is in the inception stage, offering an opportunity for all to deeply reflect on the problem and keeping in mind the people are most affected.

The concern with prevention and redressal reflected in the literature has not been concretized in to policies and programmes, as seen in the responses of government agencies or civil society. While plenty of recommendations have been made, translating them into programmes on the around has not been an easy task. Formulating effective policies becomes all the more difficult because of the association of trafficking with other extreme forms of exploitation. This requires a much greater effort on the part of the concerned agencies than what has been reported in the literature. The biggest hindrance to this, we believe, is the lack of a baseline study for the country, which makes an in-depth analysis of the issues involved. Literature on trafficking in India is completely dominated by the issue of commercial sexual exploitation, so much so that trafficking as a distinct crime does not get highlighted. At times is almost reduced to insignificance in comparison to commercial sexual exploitation. Even though there seems to be considerable information available, one is unable to form a picture which reflects the reality of trafficking in women and children in India.

NOTES & REFERENCES

1 For an elaboration of the definition and the various terms used, see Jordan (2002)

2. See United Nations (2000), Doezema (2002)

3. *Times of India*, 24 June 2002

4. 'Up to March 1999, 290,340 bonded labourers had been identified by the state governments; of these, 243,375 had been released and rehabilitated, some 20,000 had either died or migrated to other parts, and 17,000 were in the process of being rehabilitated' (ILO 2002b).

5. *Pioneer* 24 Hune 2002

6. *Indian Express* (Delhi) edition 16 and 30 May 2003; *Hindustan Times*, 17 June 2003; *The Hindu*, 17 February 2003; *Statesman*, 13 2003.

7. *The Hindustan Times*, 20 June 2003.

8. There is an integral connection between HIV/AIDS, gender and trafficking (UNDP 2002).

9. *Tribune*, 5 July 2003.

10. *India Today*, 28 July 2003.

3

Women and Child Trafficking in India

India is a source, destination and transit country for men, women, and children trafficked for the purpose of forced labour and commercial sexual exploitation. Internal forced labour may constitute India's largest trafficking problem; men, women, and children in debt bondage are forced to work in industries such as brick kilns, rice mills, agriculture and embroidery factories. Although no comprehensive study of forced and bonded labour has been carried out, some NGO estimate this problems affects tens of millions of Indians. Those from India's most disadvantaged social economic strata are particularly vulnerable to forced or bonded labour and sex trafficking. Women and girls are trafficked within the country for the purpose of commercial sexual exploitation and forced marriage. Children are also subjected to forced labour as factory workers, domestic servants, beggars, and agricultural workers. In recent years, there has been an increase of sex trafficking to medium-sized cities and satellite town of large cities. What we know is that poverty drives sex trafficking, and that sex trafficking as the delivery system for prostitution means that each day scores of young, poor women and girls will turn to sex trafficking and prostitution as a means to provide for themselves, and for their families, because they have no other choice. The hope is that funds earmarked for fighting poverty will eventually fight sex trafficking, too putting an end to this exploitative practice by offering viable economic options for poverty-stricken women and girls in developing nations who want to work.

India is also a destination for women and girls from Nepal and Bangladesh trafficked for the purpose of commercial sexual exploitation. There are also victims of labour trafficking among the thousands of Indians who migrate willingly every year to the Middle East, Europe, and the United States for work as domestic servants and low-skilled laborers. In some cases, such workers are the victims of fraudulent recruitment practices committed in India that lead them directly into situations of forced labour, including debt bondage; in other cases, high debts incurred to pay recruitment fees leave them vulnerable to exploitation by unscrupulous employers in the destination countries, where some are subjected to conditions of involuntary servitude, including non-payment of wages, restrictions on movement, unlawful withholding of passports, and physical or sexual abuse. Men and women from Bangladesh and Nepal are trafficked through India for forced labour and commercial sexual exploitation in the Middle East. Over 500 Nepali girls were jailed in the state of Bihar on charges of using false documents to transit India in the pursuit of employment in Gulf countries. Indian nationals travel to Nepal and within the country for child sex tourism.

The Government of India does not fully comply with the minimum standards for the elimination of trafficking; however, it is making significant efforts to do so. Despite these significant efforts, India has not demonstrated sufficient progress in its law enforcement efforts to address human trafficking, particularly bonded labour; therefore, India is placed on Tier 2 Watch List. India's central government faces several challenges in demonstrating a more robust anti-trafficking effort: states under the Indian Constitution have the primary responsibility for law enforcement and state-level authorities are limited in their abilities to effectively confront interstate and transnational trafficking crimes; complicity in trafficking by many Indian law enforcement officials and overburdened courts impede effective prosecutions; widespread poverty continues to provide a huge source of vulnerable people; and the Indian government faces other equally pressing priorities such as basic healthcare, education, and counterterrorism. During the reporting period, the central government continued to improve coordination among a multitude of bureaucratic agencies that play a role in anti-trafficking and labour issues. Government authorities continued to rescue victims of trafficking for commercial sexual exploitation and forced child labour. Several state governments (Andhra Pradesh, Bihar, Maharashtra, Goa, and West Bengal) demonstrated significant efforts in prosecution, protection, and prevention, although largely in the area of trafficking for commercial sexual exploitation.

Sex trafficking is big business, second only to drug and gun trafficking throughout the world. The U.S. government estimates that criminals are making $9.5 billion a year from sex trafficking.[1] Going after the criminals who exploit women and girls has proved less than successful, as the trade has continued to grow. For sex trafficking to be halted requires a two-front war: going after the criminals, and addressing the poverty factor that motivates sex trafficking in the first place.

The fact that sex trafficking is a direct product of poverty is a widely recognized truth by humanitarian organizations, governments and academic researchers. The United States Agency for International Development (USAID) says: "Trafficking is inextricably linked to poverty. Wherever privation and economic hardship prevail, there will be those destitute and desperate enough to enter into the fraudulent employment schemes that are the most common intake systems in the world of trafficking."[2]

Commissioned by UNICEF in October of 2005 to do an unprecedented study of post-war children in Bosnia-Herzegovina, lead researcher and Fulbright scholar Ann Janette Rosga found that the post-war poverty many of these children were living in directly led them into sex trafficking situations. She commented on her findings:

> *People often think that all child sex traffickers kidnap their victims, but in many cases the children end up funneled into the system by their own* families because of extreme poverty. Sometimes the children leave home *voluntarily because of abuse or other harmful conditions. Very often it's not organized criminals but close relatives or family friends who encourage girls in poverty-stricken families to seek work abroad as an 'au pair or waitress.' These acquaintances know full well that the girl will be put to work*

> *as a prostitute and that they will directly profit from the 'referral,' Furthermore, it's not uncommon for girls to know what they're entering into, and to enter voluntarily to some degree. Maybe they think they'll be different and able to escape, or maybe they'd rather take the risk than feel powerless staying at home in poverty.*[3]

In the Philippines where land development government contracts are displacing rural families, it is estimated that up to 40% of the sex workers in larger Philippine cities are from these rural areas, forced to leave their homes and find work elsewhere. The only people profiting from these exploited women and girls are the traffickers, the bar and brothel owners and the government who touts their young sex workers as a tourist attraction.[4]

From a recent article in the Philippine newspaper the *Sun Star,* Jun Malig writes of young, desperate Filipinas being trafficking to Japan for prostitution:

> The real danger of becoming an unwilling victim of human trafficking syndicates turns into a minor concern of a young woman who is desperate enough to hoist her family from the vicious cycle of poverty. Illusions and dreams frequently prevail over life's sad realities, especially in the youthful mind of someone very eager to escape from material deprivation. Many are prepared to face any form of consequences if only to free their families from the clutches of poverty.[5]

In Kenya, where severe drought has driven many rural dwellers into the cities to seek work, a disturbing trend has recently developed. AllAfrica.com reports:

> *...parents have resorted to sending their young daughters into the towns to trade their bodies for money to feed their families. "Because food reserves have run out and mothers can no longer afford to feed their children, many decide that the only way out is to 'go to the street',"* said Iris Krebber, regional coordinator of the NGO, German Agro Action. *"Many times, the girls are as young as twelve."*[6]

A report on the sex trafficking of children in Kenya released in June by UNICEF highlights the findings that more than 1,500 girls under the age of 18 are working as prostitutes or in bars in the Coast Province. "Our study shows that *boda boda* men (bicycle tax operators), beach operators, taxi drivers, police and even hotel and guest house owners are playing pimps in support of child sex tourism," says the report. The report blames parents "who are encouraging their children to practise prostitution when they are as young as 12 years."

Continuing from this article from Nairobi's newspaper, *The Nation*, addressing this report:

The deputy director of children's services in the Ministry of Home Affairs, Ms Margaret Basigwa, challenged the society to freely discuss issues affecting children and families, to have a lasting solution to the problem.

According to this report, parents have a role to play. And other Kenyans are to ensure that issues of children's rights, poverty and families are urgently addressed, she said, adding that figures showed that most children who participated in commercial sex were either orphans or from broken families.[7]

While factors such as gender discrimination organized crime syndicates, conflict are regional natural disasters all contribute greatly to the increase of sex trafficking within a particular area, the single greatest contributing factor to sex trafficking is poverty.

The poorest countries in the world are also some of the countries most affected by or involved in sex trafficking - either as countries of origin, transit or destination.

In countries where women cannot work because of a depressed economy and therefore, a lack of employment opportunities, many will turn to sex trafficking and prostitution as a means to feed themselves and their families. And many families will sell their young daughters to traffickers because they are so desperate for money.

Small grant programs for women that enable them to start regional cooperatives or their own businesses have been successful in improving the quality of life for poor women. The World Bank has focused grant money in poor rural areas of China and South

America where women often make up more than 50% of the populations there. Giving women the opportunity to work in a cooperative or to start their own business, not only provides money for themselves and their families, but it increases their self-esteem, their visibility and respect within a community and the incidence of domestic violence and sexually exploitation is also greatly decreased.

Child Trafficking is a ghastly reality that stares in the face of the civilized global community. India is not free from the clutches of this social vice. Child trafficking is rampant in India and the Indian government despite undertaking several measures has not been able to root out this horrible social menace completely. Every year thousands of children are trafficked and are forced to serve as bonded laborers and slaves. The girl children fall prey to the prostitution rackets and land in the brothels or end up being sex slaves. Some of them are forced to work as domestic servants. The internet is abuzz with portals on child trafficking. www.bestindiansites.com has collated the top Indian portals offering comprehensive information on child trafficking in India.

Child trafficking is a bitter reality that stares in the face of the civilized human society. A survey conducted by a voluntary organization found Varanasi to be the main child-trafficking hub of India. Varanasi is considered as a highly sacred Indian city and is the major pilgrim spot of India. It beggars belief that this sacred city can act as the main child-trafficking hub of India. But if the results of this survey are anything to go by then this sacred Indian city is serving as the main child-trafficking junction of India. This news portal hosts an article detailing the results of the survey carried out by that voluntary organization. The Human Welfare Association, a non-government organization was offered the first project to make the people of Uttar Pradesh aware about this social vice and to devise strategies to fight this social menace. This project is supported by the Indo German Social Service Society. The director of the Human Welfare Association, Dr. Rajnikant estimated that around 65% of the inmates who are lodged in the remand homes in Mumbai hail from the districts of Bihar, Madhya Pradesh and Uttar Pradesh. It also found that over 50,000 children and adolescent girls hailing from Nepal are trafficked to cities like Kolkata, Delhi, Goa and Mumbai every year through Varanasi. Visit this site and acquaint yourself with this growing social menace. You will get a complete picture of the child trafficking in India by reading this article.[8]

An ugly reality stares in the face of the Indian society today and this is child trafficking. Child trafficking is an unbearable social menace. Child trafficking is a curse to the society. India has tried to fight this evil but with little progress. India still remains in the tier 2 watch list for the fourth year in a row. This ranking denotes that India is not complying with the standards that the U.S. had laid down for combating child trafficking. The Trafficking in Persons or the TIP report assesses the steps undertaken by the different countries to curb human trafficking and this report is released every year by the State department of the U.S. The report of the previous year found India as the source, destination and also the transit country for human trafficking. The report cited that the Indian government was not able to investigate and prosecute human and child trafficking rackets in India. Reacting to the TPI report the Government of India undertook numerous steps to improve this condition and established a special cell within the Ministry of Home Affairs to solve the problem and to create a policy for vigorously implementing the "Immoral Traffic Prevention Act". The "Bureau of Police Research and Development" brought out the Human Trafficking Handbook for Investigators to train the police force for combating this social evil. It has been decided that certain amendments will be made in the Immoral Traffic Act and the Indian Ministry of Women and Child Development are chalking out elaborate schemes to prevent human trafficking and to rescue and provide rehabilitation for the victims of human trafficking. Log onto this web address and go through this highly informative piece of article on child trafficking. You will get an in-depth insight into the human trafficking in India by reading this exclusive article.[9]

Children are trafficked and then are forced into various types of illegitimate work. The practice of child trafficking is an extension of the human slavery that was banned about a century ago. The now-defunct practice of human slavery is carried forward by the ghastly trade of child trafficking. Check-out the reports of international surveys conducted on child trafficking that are presented on this portal. For the last couple of decades there has been a considerable rise in the cases of child trafficking. It is estimated that over 800,000 people are smuggled across the international borders every year and the majority of these (about 50%) trafficked population consists of children. Child trafficking is growing at an alarming rate in India. The U.S. State Department estimates that more than 200,000 people are either trafficked into or are smuggled through India. Go through this article and acquire in-depth information on child trafficking in India.[10]

Women and child becoming vulnerable to trafficking as they were unable to survive with dignity because of lack of livelihood options. Trafficking has been an area of concern since the early 20th century but it especially attracted attention during the 1980's. More recently, there has been a widening of its focus. However, this was not accompanied by as independent and sustained mass movement, against trafficking in the country. In the absence of awareness of human rights, the economically and socially deprived people at the grassroots have became easy prey to the trafficking trade. Migrating population have become most vulnerable to exploitation by traffickers. Its mainly the women, children and poor people from rural area who are the victims of trafficking. Trafficked persons are reportedly traumatized by their experience. Depression and suicidal thoughts are commonly reported. The mental emotional state of the survivors may include malevolence, helplessness and withdrawal, disassociation, self blame and identification with the aggressor, whereby the victims convince themselves that their experiences had to happen instead of viewing them as traumatic. Some of the psychiatric disordered among survivors of trafficking are listed as post traumatic stress disorder, depressive disorder, dissociative disorder, psychotic disorder and eating. Girls are made to bear the responsibility of upholding the family honours through their sexual purity/ chastity. If they are trafficked into commercial sexual exploitation, they face additional stress because of the prevalent morality.

The crime of trafficking involves the violation of a whole gamut of laws and human right specially women and child rights. It becomes a threat to society because traffickers operate across borders with impunity, with the growing involvement of organized criminals and by generally undermining the rule of law. Trafficking 'threaten the very fabric of society' because it involves not only criminals but also law enforcers.[11] India is a source, destination and transit country for men, women, and children trafficked for the purpose of forced labour and commercial sexual exploitation. The 2010 trafficking in person report observed that in recent years, there has been an increased of sex trafficking to sub cities and India is a destination for women and girls from Nepal and Bangladesh for the purpose of commercial sexual exploitation. Despite being an affected country, India lacks in efforts to enforce law to tackle human trafficking of men, women, and children. As per the women and child development estimate, 3 million women in India fall prey to trafficking annually in the country and 40 percent of these are minors. It is not the case with India only but "human Trafficking" is a global issue of serious concern, which causes a gross violation of human rights. India's record of prevention of trafficking in persons remains abysmally poor. Andhra Pradesh, West Bengal, Maharastra, Tamil Nadu, Karnataka, Bihar, Orissa and Delhi are said to have been identified as the most affected states. At the cross-border level, the majority victims trafficked into India for the purpose of commercial sexual exploitation belong to Nepal and Bangladesh.

Among the state where children under 16 were found in brothels, the number was highest in Bihar, followed by Maharastra and Uttar Pradesh. Among the states with the highest number of girls in the 16-17 age group, Andhra Pradesh comes first with 128 girls, followed by Uttar Pradesh and Karnataka. In needs to be mentioned here that in many places, there was a deliberate attempt by brothel owners to project the victims of commercial sexual exploitation as adult and thus downplay the number of children in the 'trade'. This was true of states like Goa and Delhi, where because of the intervention of the high courts and NGO activism, brothel owners were aware that keeping a person under 18 years in a brothel is by itself a crime. I would like to highlight here some of the major trafficking supply state.

Karnataka:[12] A report by Shakti Vahini (2004) confirms that Karnataka, where Odanadi is located, as one of the major trafficking supply states. There is a high volume of trafficking to tourist destinations such as Goa and Mumbai. It is estimated that 45% of the prostitutes in Mumbai are from Karnataka. 15% of trafficked women who were interviewed in a study carried out by UNIFEM were trafficked from Karnataka; the second highest total after Andra Pradesh (Sen, A. 2005: A Report on Trafficking of Women and Children, UNIFEM).

Karnataka is also in the "devadasi belt". Devadasi is a traditional cultural practice in which a woman / girl is 'dedicated' to a God. Although illegal in Karnataka, the practice continues and provides a front by which trafficking can be legitimised

A 2005 study by UNIFEM (Sen, A. 2005: A Report on Trafficking of Women and Children, UNIFEM) which interviewed victims of trafficking for commercial sexual exploitation who had been rescued found that:

- They were forced to service an average of seven clients a day. They could not exercise choice with regards to wearing condoms or other safe sex practices. 30% were suffering from a sexually transmitted disease; 8% had contracted HIV
- 20% were children aged below 18 years of age, the majority of which had been trafficked at a very young age.
- 57% of them had been previously arrested by the police but were not offered any support or rehabilitation so were forced to return to brothels
- 60% were also victims of child marriage
- 45.6% had their first sexual experience under the age of 16,
- 22% had been working in a brothel when they were aged less than 16

- 68% were lured into brothels with the promise of jobs
- 50% of the traffickers interviewed for the study focused on rural areas for recruitment, targeting communities which are particularly vulnerable, due to lack of employment, illiteracy, social and gender discrimination

West Bengal:[13] A study conducted by Save the Children in collaboration with the state Department of Women and Child Development and Social Welfare has categorised three trafficking-prone blocks in the state—Patharpratima and Sandeshkhali I and II.

While Sandeshkhali I and II comprise eight gram panchayats each, covering 178 villages, the Patharpratima block has 15 gram panchayats covering 87 villages.

"The study shows that these blocks are the most vulnerable ones. An increase in the child trafficking cases in the state is alarming which need immediate attention of the government," said Save the Children state head Manabendra Nath Ray.

The study revealed that in 265 villages of the state, 3,429 children had left home to work in urban centers and 271 of them are still missing. According to the report, while 82.92 per cent of children left home for work, 48.36 per cent had been lured out of their homes on the pretext of marriage or work by agents. 32.38 per cent were sent with neighbours and relatives and only 7.79 per cent ran away from home.

The NGO took into account police records to gather the data on missing children.

Only 16.18 per cent of the cases were reported to the police or the panchayat while in 83.82 per cent of the cases parents tried to get information on their own. In 29.82 per cent cases the parents feared the police and 11.84 per cent of them expressed a lack of faith in the police.

In contrast to the NGO report, the National Crime Records Bureau website displays information about 149 missing children—142 from Sandeshkhali and seven from Patharpratima.

The study said that 71 children had been reported missing since 2005 in Patharpratima alone, for which a general diary or FIR had been registered.

Data from the Sandeshkhali police station revealed that from 2004 to 2006, as many as 302 children were reported missing with only 30 children having been traced during this period.

The study pegged the percentage of missing girls to 66.67 per cent and of missing boys to 33.33 per cent. While 49.06 per cent were between the age of 15 and 18 years, 29.96 per cent were between 13 to 14 years of age and 20.97 per cent were below 12 years of age.

Further, while 15.04 per cent of missing children had never attended school, 76.69 per cent had completed the fifth standard. Among girls, 64.61 per cent had attended school up to the third standard, while 14.61 per cent had never attended school.

In the report, Delhi surfaces as the favoured destination of child traffickers, followed by Kolkata, Bihar and Uttar Pradesh.

While 72.77 per cent of the respondents attributed absence of communication as the reason to ascertain that the child was missing, in 17.41 per cent of cases the child just left home and did not return.

Trafficking in women follows a certain pattern in most of the cases. The trafficking figures are high in West Bengal as the state has more of rural population than urban. The traffickers mostly target women and children who belong to the rural areas. Trafficking in women is most prominent in the southern part of South 24 Parganas, the eastern part of Murshidabad, the eastern side of Nadia, and the eastern region of North 24 Parganas. The traffickers, often known to the families, act as agents who offer lucrative jobs to the young women, and promise to take them to the cities. The women are often vulnerable, and are tempted by the agents to leave their families and join them for "work". Sometimes, the parents themselves hand over their daughters to the agents. The agents often escort the girls to a suburban railway station, and take them to far-off cities like Mumbai, Pune, Hyderabad, Bangalore and Delhi. Immediately after the women reach these cities, the girls are forced into "Commercial Sexual Exploitation".

The families of the girls get no inkling of what is happening to the girls, as the agents send money to the families for 4-5 months, claiming it to be the money sent by the girls. When after a few months, the families stop receiving money and news about the girl's wellbeing, the family members begin to worry and lodge a missing diary at the local police station. Getting a tip-off from the local police stations, the CID takes charge, and tries to trace the missing girls. After her gruesome experience, a child is traumatised, and finds it difficult to get used to a normal life".

Orissa: The increasing events of women trafficking in Orissa has set alarm bell ringing towards the law-and-order condition.[14] According to sources, girls and women belonging to economically backward sections of the coastal Orissa and the poor of tribal-dominated western Orissa are regularly supplied out of the state. Taking the advantage of their poverty and simplicity, the brokers trap them in their net by giving false promises of marriage, job and so on.

The police has been able to rescue about 238 married, 394 maidens and 429 minor girls during these five years. On the other hand, the number of the missing girls is increasing year-by-year. In the year 2000, about 449 women were reportedly missing but in 2001 this number increased to 608. In 2003, the number increased to 996 and 923 women were reportedly missing during 2005. As per the report, the ratio of missing is high in case of minor children, who are easily trapped by the brokers in their net.

Irregularity halts primary education in Western Orissa

While the government is spending crores of rupees on different welfare programmes for the development of tribal people in the KBK districts of Orissa, the modus operandi hardly achieves the goal. The brightest example is Nawrangapur district. Nawrangpur is one of the tribal-dominated districts of the state where about 65 per cent people are tribal. For their all-round development, the government is running different programmes and education is one of them. The Department of Tribal Rural Welfare (TRW) of the state government monitors the education programmes in the village schools. But it is unable to hit the target due to severe corruption, irregularities and embezzlement of funds.

According to official sources, about 224 schools including 14 high schools for boys, five kanya ashrams, one girl high school, 42 residential schools, 14 service centers, and 146 primary school hostels are being run by the government in this district. But these schools are affected with deficiency of teaching staff. Out of 146 primary schools, about 90 of them are awaiting adequate number of teaching staff. The hostels are also crying for proper attention and improvement. In most of the hostels, the inmates suffer from the lack of basic amenities. The students have no adequate dresses, mosquito nets and are not supplied with blankets, though the administration claims to have supplied them. Many students still suffer from malnutrition due to inadequacy of balanced food. However, the government has arranged for Rs. 300 as stipend for each student each month. But, it hardly benefits the real beneficiaries. Most of the institutions allegedly show more enrolment in the records to get more funds as stipend money and it has become a good way for easy income in this district. The mid-day meal programme has also been crippled due to massive corruption.

Five minor tribal boys from Rayagada district were rescued by the railway police from the railway station at Bangalore on 13th February. All the boys are in their teen belong to Hikriguda and Mardijhola villages from Dumernali Panchayt under Bissam-Cuttack block in Rayagada district. According to the statement of the rescued boys, a person called Madhav has allured them for migration to south in order to earn better wage and lifestyle. He first brought these boys by a truck to Rayagada and later boarded a train to Balugam in Orissa. Afterward, a person named Gandhi has appeared at Balugam and accompanied the boys throughout the train journey to Bangalore. None of the boys had any idea as where they are heading towards.

The group arrived in Bangalore on the early hours of 13th

February and while the boys were waiting at the railway station platform, the police got suspicious and detained the children and quizzed to know the reason behind their coming to Bangalore. Since the children were unable to understand any language other than Oriya, the boys were later handed over to the CWC, Child Welfare Committee, under the Women and Child Development department of Govt. of Karnataka and shifted to the Children's home.

The CWC has published the details about the children in the local news paper in Bangalore. Based on the news, Concern for Working Children, a Bangalore based NGO has visited the Balamandira (children's home) and seek to interact with the children but fail to communicate with them because of language problem. Subsequently, the CWC informed Migration Information Resource Centre (MiRC) Aide et Action, Bhubaneswar to help establishing communication with the boys to know their details. Consequently we have requested one Mr. Kamaskhi Panda from Orissa who stays in Bangalore to help communicating with the children. Now CWC has been able to access all details about the boys and communicated to MIRC. Immediately the information were passed on to the local press and the District Collector of Rayagada for appropriate action. Information last reaching indicates that, the parents of the boys have been informed and attempt are being made to facilitate safe return of the boys.

This issue is not an isolated case where children's are being lured and taken to far off place to work in various hazardous industries like, poultry, seed farms, apparel factories, domestic work and various such sectors where the labour of the child can be exploited. The Government of India is coming up with ICPS (Integrated Child Protection Service) in line with ICDS to take proactive measures to protect the rights of the children. This will allow the government to set up child rights protection committees and keep a vigil on movement of children to other states and coordinate joint operation with other State government and district to rescue and rehabilitate the victims.

Andhra Pradesh: Andhra Pradesh has achieved the dubious distinction of leading the other states in trafficking in females, says a survey by Prajwala, a non-governmental organization.[15] Andhra Pradesh has emerged as the largest supplier of women and children for sexual exploitation (refer National Human Rights Report 2001, USAID Report & National Commission for Women study in 1997). These and other surveys also concluded that 25% of all trafficked victims are children. It witnesses both inter and intra state trafficking. It supplies women and girl children to different cities/towns of India for prostitution and also sends across the borders to the Middle East countries for the same. Andhra Pradesh is also a state with the highest prevalence of HIV/AIDS affected and infected persons.[16]

25-85% of women in prostitution in other cities/metros belong traditionally to Andhra Prdesh The percentage of Andhra Pradesh Girls and women in four cities: Delhi - 45%, Mumbai - 28%, Kolkota - 3%, Goa- 80%.and also Lattur, Yavatmal, Chandrapur, Bangalore, Chennai and Mahabalipuram show the extent of the trafficking from AP. It shows that there are large number of women and children trafficked into cities and towns a across the country from Andhra Pradesh. (Field studies on inter-state trafficking for Commercial Sexual Exploitation from Andhra Pradesh - A situation Report by Jose Vetticatil and Sunitha Krishnan supported by CRS).

In Andhra Pradesh , Coastal regions of the state more than 26% of the women or girls entered into prostitution between the age of 14-16 years, 20% between 16-18 years and 16% before the age of 14 years. Against the widely accepted definition of a child as one below 18years of age, more that 60% of the victims are subjected to sexual exploitation as children. (Status of Sex-workers & their children in Coastal Andhra Pradesh. A recent study conducted by HELP-Ongole in AP. supported by Action Aid).

Apart from trafficking, within AP Traditional forms of prostitution are prevalent: Joginis, Mathammas (Basivi), Dommara, Kallavanthulus and Yerukalasani etc. Children and especially girls who are child laboureres or are bonded are directly at a risk of being sexually exploited.

About 70% of victims come from the Scheduled castes, and backward castes. Almost all are poor, desperately so, A sizeable number are tribals. The root causes of trafficking are multiple and complex. There are several factors responsible for child trafficking. Some are cultural and religious, while others can be traced to economic causes; especially in those resulting in the face of liberalization and globalization. Sometimes it becomes difficult to distinguish between cause and purposes of trafficking. A deep-rooted social stratification within the Indian society means that children belonging to the underprivileged sections are the most vulnerable. The impact of globalization and liberalization in increasing poverty, unemployment and forced migration, disintegration of the family, growing consumerism, trafficking has become a lucrative business. The growing commodification of women and children, makes them vulnerable to being trafficked.

Many children are thrust into prostitution networks by their families - an unpleasant fact, but true. Not all poor parents sell off their daughters, of course; some may be victims of pimps and agents posing as grooms of employers. But many do it knowingly. A UNICEF report on child prostitution in India confirms this, stating that " family members of girls? acting, independently?. Execute a sizeable percentage of total trafficking operations."

A systematic organised trafficking network of wealthy, experienced individuals buy, transport and sell children into prostitution. It must however be noted that trafficking is prevalent at various levels — local, inter-district, inter-state and cross-border. Inter state trafficking is smaller than local and inter-district trafficking. Cross-border trafficking from AP, mostly occur in the form of contract marriages to the Middle East.

Rajasthan: Violence committed against women is very high in Rajasthan.[17] Evil practices like the demand and acceptance of dowry is widespread in the state. The practice of payment of dowry is more rampant within the middleclass society. Even highly educated women from prestigious institutions are married off to strangers against their will. One of the well known womençe colleges in the state has a considerable number of dropouts in their higher degree courses since their students are often forced into marriages, often against their will, before they complete their studies. Once married, the woman is expected to remain at home and is confined to the four walls of her husbandçe house. Higher education for women is only considered as a quotient to bargain for less dowry in the middleclass society in Rajasthan.

The Dowry Prohibition Act, 1961 prohibits the demand and acceptance of dowry in India. However, if the Act is to be implemented, and the practice of dowry to be rooted out, what the state requires is good policing and a criminal justice system that functions. But in the state where women are treated as chattels, valued at par with cattle, the execution of the Act has failed. One has only to look at the records of the National Crime Records Bureau. Cases registered against the demand and acceptance of dowry in Rajasthan are relatively low in comparison to other cases of violence committed against women across the country.

Criminal acts, like verbal, emotional and physical abuse of women within the home is not considered as a crime in the state. Even courts reject complaints filed by women complainants on the ground that a woman does not have a right to complain, particularly if the complaint is against her husband or any other relative. This situation gives a handle to criminals abusing women.

Women are often compelled to engage in drug trafficking and prostitution in Rajasthan. Women forced into such activities are abducted from rural villages at a very young age, trained in distant places and later forced into active service. Several of them who get caught by the law enforcement agencies at a later stage in their career end up in state prisons. Those who get arrested remain in prison for years without any recourse to legal or medical aid. Many are raped in custody. Not being able to complain about their situation they end up as carriers of life-threatening diseases and other sexually transmitted ailments.

The commonly heard excuse for this dismal condition of women in Rajasthan is the feudal mindset of the society in that state. Even though it is true to a certain extent that several persons in Rajasthan indeed entertain a feudal mindset, the actual cause for the uninterrupted continuation of violence against the women in Rajasthan is the failure of the law enforcing agencies to maintain rule of law in the state.

In many parts of the state, the law enforcement agency, particularly the police, are controlled by the local political party leaders. Most of them, believing and propagating their interpretation of Hinduism, promoted by the Bharatiya Janata Party [BJP] advocate Manu's proposition of women being equated to a Dalit. According to Manu law, the *Manusmriti*, women do not have equal status vis a vis the men. They have no other right other than those that have been granted to them by their husbands.

The local police are controlled by the political henchmen who are in turn motivated by the interpretation of Hinduism as dictated by the BJP, the ruling party of the state. This is the cause for the blatant refusal of the police to register complaints by women and women groups in the state for crimes committed against them. Anyone who is adamant is referred to the local political party leader or the party office. Such referrals often result in further abuse, often in public, which serves as a powerful deterrent against any woman or group, who is already isolated within the society. The courts in Rajasthan are also not free from a similar influence.

Continuing violence against a particular section in the society does not happen in a vacuum. There are several factors that facilitate such unfettered continuation of evil practices. In the state of Rajasthan, a corrupt law enforcement mechanism including a non- independent judiciary is the key factor that has sanctioned the unabated recurrence of barbaric crimes against women. The religiously charged political ideology that leads the state administration is just the veil covering an almost fallen system in which the women in Rajasthan continue to be persecuted within the confines of their own family.

This is the situation in almost all the state of India. If this continues, no girls in the poor rural area will be safe and this is a direct violation of women's and child right to life also. This heart-rending fact is pointing to the truth that, the status of women is looming in dark in few states and it is casting shadow over other poverty stricken states like Orissa, Bihar where young girls are becoming victim to arbitrary marriage, trafficking and sexual exploitation, inhuman mental and physical torture - in a word facing extreme violation of human right. Every year hundreds of girls are married out to unknown future. Even parent/family does not bother to follow up them. This happened mostly in poorest of families with grown up girls of so called high cast society. The crime of trafficking involves the violation of a whole gamut of laws and human rights. Trafficking 'threatens the very fabric of society' because it involves not only criminals but also law enforcers. To go straight to the root cause of sex trafficking means many years of research to identify these trafficked populations, many years of work to improve the economies and well-being of these impoverished areas, perhaps many years to earn the trust of these vulnerable women and girls, many years to follow through while these affected nations begin a rise out of poverty and primarily, a great amount of money to develop programs that provide an alternative to sex trafficking and address poverty as the root cause of sex trafficking.

NOTES & REFERENCES

1. U.S. Women Without Borders. "We Mobilize to Address Modern Day Slavery." October 25, 2005.
2. IOM International Organization for Migration. *Trafficking in Migrants: Quarterly Bulletin* No 23 - April 2001 - Special Issues.
3. Medical News Today. March 1, 2005. "Child sex-trafficking study in Bosnia reveals misperceptions."
4. Monte, Janice Lee. GABRIELA News and Features, 25 February 1999. "Across borders: Sex trafficking of women."
5. Malig, Jun A. SunStar Pampanga. "Malig: "Unqualified Japan-bound entertainers?" July 4, 2006.
6. United Nations Office for the Coordination of Humanitarian Affairs – Integrated Regional Information Networks (IRIN) "Kenya: Drought, poverty forcing young women into risky commercial sex". March 29, 2006
7. Namlola, Juma. The Nation (Nairobi), "Kenya: 1,500 Underage Girls in Sex Trade, Says Unicef." June 23, 2006
8. Indiatimes.com

9. Indianexpress.com \

10. bba.org.in

11. http://www.indiansocialstudy.com

12. http://www.odanadi-uk.org/about-odanadi/trafficking/trafficking-karnataka.html

13. http://www.expressindia.com

14. http://www.organiser.org/

15. http://www.rediff.com/news/2002(sep/19iefi.htm)

16. http://www.helpap.in/Trafficking.html

17. http://www.wluml.org/node/3932

4

Women and Child Trafficking in North-Eastern India

Trafficking of women and children from the North-eastern states of India and the bordering countries in the North-east is a serious issue but has so far not drawn public attention.

North-east region of India consists of seven states Assam, Arunachal Pradesh, Mizoram, Nagaland, Meghalaya, Manipur and Tripura. It has a long international border with Bangladesh on the west, Myanmar (Burma) in the east and China and Bhutan on the north. It is connected with rest of the country through narrow passage. Assam serves as a gateway for the other six states to reach to other parts of India.

Trafficking in Northeast region occurs at two levels there is the internal trafficking of children and women from conflict affected rural areas for domestic work and prostitution. Secondly, on an international level, there is trafficking of women to other South East Asian countries the Bangladesh, Bhutan, Bangkok, via Myanmar (Burma) for various purposes, such as drug trafficking, labour, bar girl and prostitution.

The term 'internal trafficking' was not an issue in North East region recently. In the year 2003 onwards it was addressed by the initiatives of some social organizations. The awareness building and rescue intervention carried out along with the drug trafficking in border district made internal trafficking as subject of growing concern. There is no study on the subject in the context of eight Northeastern regions on internal trafficking of women and children. The internal trafficking does exist in the border district of North-east region. Amongst the 60 CSWS interviewed in Nagaland, Dimapur and Assam border indicates growing menace of internal trafficking of girls in the region.[1] Besides this luring women and children in the name of providing domestic work in metro cities are growing particularly in the conflict affected areas such as Bodoland Territorial Council, Assam. There are 109 girls lured from the relief camps of Srirampur gate under Kokrajhar district of BTC, Assam for domestic work in many parts of the country and outside of the country such as Bhutan and Nepal. No study has been carried out so far on young girls working in bar, cabin restaurant. It is prevalent in the bordering areas of North East region with other South East Asian countries. According to the international definition any girls below the age of 18 transported into prostitution has to be trafficked. In the northeast region, significant numbers of girls working as unorganized bar, restaurants are under the age of 18. Thus the have been trafficked.[2] The growing number of girls working as bar restaurant girls in many trans-border areas of North-east are due to the conflict, poverty and flood situation adding with looking for glamorous world. There is no particular caste or community only working in such areas, but all section of the community from North-east region.

The combination of poverty, ethnic conflict, unemployment, gender inequality (the low status of girl children) inadequate legislation and law enforcement enables trafficking in girls to thrive in north-east. It is a general practice of the poor family to send their children work in the wealthy family in the urban or rural areas. Today this practice has been exploited by the trafficker to lure the children, especially girls to supply for those wealthy family looking for the domestic labour. These children generally do not have access to any kind of education, freedom and working long hours to fulfill the owners demand in the poor unhygienic condition with primarily no pay. It is also fact that not all the girls who migrate in the urban areas are trafficked. In North East particularly organization stated such movement of children is not facilitated by third parties and such is not trafficking. Many girls move to urban areas in order to earn livelihood, and then find themselves living in the insecure areas and most of them are in the target of exploitation, especially commercial sexual exploitation.[3] In some cases, children's movement is facilitated usually by the friend family related, acquaintance and distance known person to the girls. Many such girls are kept in highly exploitative conditions of work (prostitution or domestic labour) suffering non-payment (or underpayment) of wages, sexual and physical abuse, long hours and no day off in a year. Children trafficked frequently suffer rape, physical abuse, are not paid or underpaid by their exploiter. Some are abducted by the clients. In addition they suffer harassment from police and local community, unplanned pregnancy and risk of HIV/AIDS and STI infection.

North-east region such as Assam, Meghalaya, Nagaland, Manipur, Mizoram, Tripura, Arunachal Pradesh including Sikkim main destination for domestic servant are Kolkata, Delhi, Mumbai and certain extend in Bangalore and Darjeeling. The mushrooming domestic servant recruitment agents coming to the region to lure girls has the clear indication of large trafficking network operating in the region. Many cases women and girls are brought by the agents through local transportation available to Siliguri and travel to different destination along with the traffickers. Often also use truckers who carry women and girls from Northeast region through 31 National highway only route connecting rest to North east states. The reporting cases of missing girls from the region reported by the parents indicates large extent of women and girls being trafficked to other metro cities of India. Migrant domestic workers often become traffickers when they are deceived as the amount of money they will earn, the working conditions and sometimes as to the type of job they will do (work does not happened as promised). In many cases, trafficked women are forced to work 18 hours a day, without any rest, are underpaid or not paid at all, are raped, beaten, threatened and locked in the houses. Such situation women suffered gross violations, complete isolation; are forbidden in from communicating with anyone, including their families. Traffickers usually target minors and Dalit women- the most oppressed group in the society. The report claims that trafficking, though not reported from many places, occurs almost every where. "The situation is worse in area that are underdeveloped. Trafficking of women and children from the North Eastern states and bordering countries – in both directions – is a serious public issue that has not drawn attention. Pangsa and Dimapur in Nagaland and Morey in Manipur are the major trans-border transit and demand centers. Women and children from Assam and Bangladesh are trafficked to Morey, and are moved out from there to Myanmar and other South East Asian countries. The long drawn conflicts in the North Eastern states have made women and children highly vulnerable.

Why are the women and girls form North-east are trafficked? There are many reasons for trafficking, some of the important reasons are prostitution, sexual purposes, smuggling, bonded labourers, entertainment industries, drugs/arms trafficking. Cheap domestic labour etc. With the advent of the security forces, prostitution has emerged as growing menace in north-east region. Added to these are the means of drugs and alcohol available in the states. Despite denial by the government authority, it is a fact that trafficking network exist, connecting to other South0east Asian countries. Local residents confirm the presence of middle men (kingpins) who deal the girls.[4] The most victims are the women and girls from the indigenous groups are especially vulnerable to trafficking in North-east region. They often do not share the language educational access or even the right to citizenship of the minority population. So they lack the economic opportunities, the knowledge and the rights, which could protect them from trafficking. It is very cleared from the statistic that 61% commercial sex workers in India belong to scheduled caste and scheduled tribes and the other backward communities. Trafficking of women for prostitution has not been documented in North-east region. Although there are cases of women who are also deceived and find themselves forced into prostitution. There is a significant movement of cross border within the region for prostitution. The cases reported of trafficking has been arising day by day from North East. More work needs to ascertained the extend of coercion in trafficking for the sex industry, as there is also clearly migration for sex work that may not been trafficking. Some report have indicated that South East Asian women especially India/North-east women trafficked to African countries under the guise of working as performers, but then are forced into prostitution.[5] Due to lack of data on trafficking, there is a lack of information on the background of trafficked women and children. Many impoverished ethic community (Adhibasi and Bodo) living in the still existing relief camps due to the ethnic conflict, rural families are willing to send their daughter away to work without regard for the risks and consequences. Orphaned girls who had lost their parents and whose relatives are languishing lives in the relief camps are thought to be especially vulnerable to trafficking and highly vulnerable to HIV/AIDS. This is a growing problem, especially in Bodoland Territorial Council (BTC), Assam and surrounding districts of Assam to BTC. Substantial number of trafficking cases is known about ethnicity of trafficked women, still need key areas for further research.

The impact of the ethnic conflict in the region except Arunachal Pradesh, Sikkim and certain extend Meghalaya has drained away the peace and development in the region. In the process of conflict women and children are the worst sufferer. The extensive internal displacement of families and individuals has increased the vulnerability of ethnic girls and women by reducing the protection of their husband or mail members of the family. The conflict has certainly increased the incident of women becoming sex workers, internal trafficking, luring the minor girls into prostitution and unsafe mobility associated vulnerability to HIV/AIDS in the region.

Insurgency, militancy or whatever name is given to the low intensity warfare in India's North East region is part and parcel of life in the region. Violence is the neutral byproduct of insurgency[6]. After effects of violence are both tangible as well as intangible. Very often the state formulates strategies to address the visible effect of violence by paying compensation to the victims or their next of kin in case of death . But while material compensation address the immediate financial need; the psychological, social and economic needs of victims who have survive deaths do not received adequate attention. Much less of plight of women who become targets of a different kind during times of conflict. There is no such institutions/NGOs documenting the such kind of heinous crime taking place amongst the women largely ethnic women in the region. While insurgency affects the life of the normal people. It has very devastating effects on women particularly ethnic women in the far-flung remote villages. But lack of documentation of the tremendous psychological and mental sufferings undergone by women in different parts of the North East region conflict situation makes difficult for the state to make appropriate interventions. Very often when peace returned, even temporarily in a certain conflict areas, there is a tendency to forget insidious effects that violence has had on women and children. Everyone believes that life goes back normal, but its certainly not. What about women and girls who are raped, tortured, by state and other non state actors? What about the women and girls who are living in the relief camps despite of the creating of the Autonomous state to the certain community. Those women does not have control over their body, sexuality and reproductive health services and no access to traditional livelihood and above all, no privacy.

When taking about insurgency and violence, it is easy to picture men, youth and old, carrying scars of gun-shots and as happened recently in Karbi Anglong Autonomous council of North East, being butchers like animals, their throat slit, their arms and leg cut into pieces their stomachs incised, the entrails out in the open. The impact of the such horror on women and children. The women needs for special attention in conflict situation is aloud enough for the policy makers to understand. Most often women and children are only target by security forces and other non state actors.

Where ever and when ever such conflict occurs in the state, women and children become the first targets of both state and non state actors because they are seen as a cultural identity of the group. Non state actors, as terrorists are called, imposed dress codes and other norms of behavior on their women. Hence they are told to be vanguards of their culture. This cultural uniqueness becomes the bandwagon for putting forward their claims to be separate homeland. This aspect has been very blatantly illustrated by insurgents of Manipur and Assam. Since the women and children are the symbol of culture in the every society of North East, state forces deployed to fight insurgency in the region also direct their attention to women and girls. They feel that if they are to deal a body blow to an insurgent movement, they must defile a defender of culture, namely the women. So the women and girls are ruthlessly raped and outraged. Such acts results in further suppression of the women as society and non state actors start regulating their movement and set timings within which their movement and beyond which they cannot venture out of their homes. Also some areas become out of bounds for some women. The social mobility of women is thus severely restricted. In case of the married women raped, she suffers multiple trauma because her family members, including her husband, consider her defiled, she develops guilt feeling and has live with that since there is hardly any social support system available in the region. Centres for counseling victims of rape and trauma are not in place in the entire North East states. Ultimately a woman has no one with whom to share her plight. There is little information connecting the conflict and post conflict situation of North East to trafficking in women and girls. Due to the unending ethnic conflict there was large-scale migration of North East women and girls to other parts of the region. From the conflict prone areas and post conflict (existing relief camps) there is a sharp increase of prostitution especially in the trans-border areas of 31 NH, the only route connecting to rest of the North East states from rest of the states. Due to lack of alternative employment opportunities and an increased demand for sexual services by truck drivers, rickshaws pullers, businessman along with the soldiers.

Patriarchy reasserts itself very strongly during times of conflict. Men see themselves as guardians of their wife, sister and daughters. Should any one be raped, molested and exploited physically, men considered it a personal lost of honor to themselves. In Nagaland and Bodolnd there are instances where men have to committed suicide because they have to watch their sister being rape by security forces. A sense of guilt follows and depression is the natural outcome. As stated above, women then forfeit heir mobility as they no longer move around after the dark. Victims of violence very often spend months and years in relief camps. The example of Kokrajhar (now Bodoland Territorial Council) and Karbi Anglong (Karbi Anglong district hills council) and Manipur. In such situations women has to suppress her sexuality and reproductive rights since situation is not normal still. The sexual relation with her husband is erratic. The woman looses her reproductive rights because she cannot prevent herself from unwanted pregnancy. Since she is compelled to give birth in a very adverse circumstances. This compounds the poverty and health problems, which are the characteristic of relief camps. Another phenomenon is that during times of conflict, militants try to exercise control over the sexuality of women, including their reproductive rights. The close watch is being kept by the militants to who she is socializing with. There are several instances where women are told they have to propagate the race and cannot practice family planning.

Women in relief camps are deprived of their traditional livelihood and they are unable to take up alternative income generating activities. The state has not evolved these lacunae. The policy of the state so far is give some ration in months and cloths to wear that is it. What state has not realize is that women and girls do not enjoy living on doles. They want to be self-sufficient. They do want to do something for the living and for the younger generation. Women in the region are skill weavers, which can bring revelution in terms of economic up-liftmen. Thousand of the girls child in the relief camps are make to sacrifice their education reasons it is unsafe for them to venture out of the camps to attend school. Relief camps does not have proper education facility. Economic reason also compelled parents to send their children out side of the states as domestic servant. But it is also fact that many schools in the vicinity of the conflict are taken over by the security forces for their temporary shelter. This further reduces the opportunity for education of girls. Nagaland and Bodoland is a good example of this form of educational exclusion. Women who lost their husband or sons to conflict s have no option but to take over the reins of the family. This change in kind compelled them to take up some kind of employment to generate resources for the family. This burdensome of the women is often very stressful and further traumatized the women. There are several female-headed household in the region due to the bliss of ethnic conflict. It might be al-right in the eyes of the larger population but children grows missing with what is the father's love is like. Most often they have to drop out to supplement the family income. This creates emotional, mental and psychological blocks that affects hem throughout their lives. No institutions so far emerged to in the North East region to help deal with the hidden trauma that such children and women suffered.

The worst hit and one of the trafficking prone areas after the twine ethnic conflict broked out within the Bodoland Territorial Council (BTC), Assam where there are trans-border existing relief camps. The reported cases are alarming by the community people and it is also clear evidence that increasing number of women soliciting sex work in and around of the NH 31 connecting to the rest of the Indian states bordering to Bhutan and having direct route to Nepal in the North and West Bengal bordering Bangladesh. More then 50 mobile sex workers have been identified. Since there is no well established red-light areas most of the sex acts are performed in the deep jungle (forest areas) in the transborder. There is a growing feared amongst the community that recently two girls died who are also mobile sex workers in that area. The sudden demised of this two girls has brought shocking and community believes that they died due to AIDS. Another migration and trafficking prone area is Deosri (Datgari) connecting direct route to Bodoland Territorial Council (BTC) Assam and Royal Kingdom of Bhutan. The area is primarily consisting of Bodo, Adhibasi and Nepalese community. The area is also hit during the ethnic conflict where thousand of the both community were internally displaced. The numbers of Adhibasi population are still living in the relief camps. This trans-border area is also prone of trafficking women and children. There has been substantial number of women and girls lured by traffickers from the areas in the pretext of providing job in the other cities. As per the report collected from the community vigilance committee (CVC) formed in the relief camps reported cases of girl child missing and most of the parents are not aware of their where about. It is also reported that parents get their daughter get married in early age due to the fear of daughter getting trafficked or rape. The situation of the area is such that girls child get married as early as at the age of 13-14 due to the fear of trafficked and rape.

The internal armed conflict in North East region has caused wide-scale trafficking of a different kind. Large numbers of children in conflict areas are recruited as comrade by the rebel forces. It is also revealed by the returnees (surrendered) girls rebel forces that most of the time they were made to performed sex to their superiors/commanders and other rebel groups leaders visiting the camps. They also informed to the authority that they were make to act sex for the blue film. Such films were made in order to raise fund to run the revel camps in the deep jungles. Most of the film made was sold to the foreign countries. It is one of the biggest blue films making network operating in the North East region. In the period from 1986-2003, approximately 3000 children were abducted, and till date 5000 children remain missing. Number of women who lost their husband during the conflict in the Kokrajhar and Chirang district of BTC alone is 300. The local administration has distributed Rs 25,000 thousand as ex-gartia for becoming widow.

Lack of employment opportunities in the NE region is also one of the root cause of the problem. Searching for employment, driven by poverty and insecurity of life has forced many women and girls to move in uncertain destination with unknown person. Many such situation the girls mobility has been trapped by the traffickers or such agents put them into the exploitative condition having without any means to return in respective home town. The poverty is the cures in North Eastern region. Adding with insurgency and natural calamity such as flood, etc. Most part of the region is still inaccessible without any transportation facility. The only means of their livelihood is small agricultural land and they depend on the agricultural alone. Most part of the region has the practiced of jhum cultivation (shifting cultivation). Many a times poor villagers borrow many from the moneylenders and till they could return the debt they become servitude to money lender. There is a possibility in certain part of the region that linkage between indebtedness and trafficking vulnerability, which need to be explored in context of North east region.

The ethnic division and monopoly of power by the dominant groups has been issue in the North Eastern region. It is the root cause of the existing problem of insurgency in the region. The development resources such as education, land, and forest have not been equally distributed and continuing marginalization of the ethnicity has resulted the region in fire for many decades. Almost 80%[7] of the NE population comprises of diverse ethnic groups, today every groups are trying hard to preserve their identity by creating self govern autonomous land. The reported case of trafficking in NE region is drawn from wide range of ethnicities including some from illegal Bangladeshis immigrants.

Women are trafficked both from urban and rural areas in context of North East region. The present mushrooming trends of trafficking in the North East is from high vulnerable ethnic women and children living in the relief camps due to the unending ethnic conflict in the region. Such situation living women and girls are more likely to be exploited more as compared to the urban and non-disturbed rural areas. Those women and girls are more vulnerable, have no access of information and less likely to complain and seek help or legal advice if in an abusive situation. Illegal agents in the pretext of domestic servant recruitment target such areas as potential place where the detection of trafficking is less. The survey conducted in the existing relief camps due to the ethnic conflict in 12 such camps revealed that the 67% of those interviewed were from Santhal/Adhibasi ethnic groups. 20% from the Bodo ethnic community and 13% are from the Bangladeshis refugees living in the BTC areas. An initial survey by NEDAN FOUNDATION of 25 women returnees found all women were in the age of between 15 to 25 years.

The vulnerability of women becomes higher during a divorce, especially for those who have children and those who are still girls themselves, having been married while underage. The marriage laws/customary laws and its associate allow men and women to divorce for the same reason. However, it puts the divorced women in a disadvantage position in terms of support from her husband after divorce. If the husband divorces his wife, the wife is entitled to get some portion of property. In NE region divorce cases are resolved within the customary laws itself. The maintenance act is rare applicable in the region. This entitlement is not applicable in terms of if the wife initiates the divorce against her husband, regardless of her reasons. The state of Meghalaya has matrilineal system. The inheritance property is registered in women name. Women status in the society is much more powerful then men. But in terms of the political system men occupied the powerful position then women despite the system of society ruled by women. Over a period of time the number of divorces cases is increasing in the region due to many reasons. Some of the reasons are practiced of bigamy, alcoholism and drug addiction. In such situation women are the victims of such worst circumstances. More then that children of the family especially girls suffered the most. Most of the time states' crisis centers are dysfunctional to help women.

The increasing cases of women becoming a widow is highlighted by many print media in the region. The factors behind is most of the women lost their husband either by rival militants groups or by Indian para-military forces with suspect that person belongs to militants group. The state having highest number of widow is reported in Assam, Manipur, Nagaland, Tripura and Mizoram. Many women after losing their bread winner in the family becomes vulnerable due to the internal circumstances and external discord. When they faced such situation in the society they lookout for dignity, justice and better livelihood due to which they often faced exploitation and injustice in the lives. One form of violence against women prevailing in certain cluster in the lower Assam is Witch Hunting. Women are branded as witch and are accused of causing harmful in the communities. These women are physically and mentally tortures and ousted from the communities. Most of the women suspected as witches are killed or buried alive. In 2005[8] alone there are 10 such reported cases of killing Bodoland Territorial Council (BTC) and Dhubri district, Assam. Control over resources, personal enmity with powerful members of the community and the prevalence of superstitions are some of the factors responsible for witch hunting. Further finding/research is needed to understand whether there are nay link between the instances of witch hunting and the ongoing ethnic conflict situation prevailing in the areas.

There are many cases of adolescent girls ignorantly pregnant. In such cases young girls are not allow to abort the child. North East region has large population belongs the Christianity and as per the beliefs system abortion is prohibited. Most of the time pregnant girls are brought to Missionary home for delivery. Once the child is delivered within few days mothers are sent back to respective villages. The missionary run adoption centers looks out for potential client to adopt the child within states and outside country. The trafficking of baby for adoption is a relatively new issue to come to public attention. There is currently not a lot of information available about the practice. Reports of the phenomenon should be read with cautions. Some of the interview conducted in our filed assessment led us to believe that many women might be voluntarily relinquishing their children for adoption, rather then being overtly coerced but are ashamed or afraid to tell the truth. This is of course still trafficking of children. Many a times mother of the child also fall prey in to prostitution.

The article 9 of the UN Conventions on the Rights of the Child stipulates that all children should be registered immediately after birth and should also acquire a name and nationality. The report calls free birth registration for all the children, adding that universal registration of all the children is a goal within the reach of the state. The unregistered and undocumented children and adults are vulnerable to exploitation. The reasons why so many children are unregistered are varied. Poor parents may find the registration fee to expensive or many poor parents are not aware of the child's registration. Rural babies are less likely to be registered compare to the urban babies. Most often rural women delivered their babies with the help of local dais or midwife. Many home birth babies goes unregistered. Lack of birth registration of children in the rural populace facilitates the trafficking of children. Agents and traffickers take due advantage of the lack of official documents to falsify the young women to work in any kinds of sectors. As per the reported cases registered in NHRC study indicates all India 40,000 children go missing[9]. It is a shocking news for the nation and it is difficult to draw a conclusion where does this children disappeared.

One dramatic manifestation of evolving alternative discourses is in the context of sexuality in North East Region. Sexuality is central social field in Northeast Region with particular attention paid to virginity of young women and find fidelity of married women. However in present scenario in fast urbanization there is an evolving sexual identity. The pre marital sex is extremely common in North East Region women and girls. The significant is the emergence of new sexual identities particularly teenage girl who may have sex with men in exchange of drugs, money. Noteworthy as well as emergent gay and lesbian sexual and political identity. The sexual culture is increasingly manifesting behaviour and tolerance to action which are untenable according to dominant social and sexual discourse. What is means in terms of trafficking is either direct, nor inevitable. The increasingly permissive sexual discourse in fast changing urban scenario in Northeast Region may contribute to the de-stigmatization of pre marital sexual activity which, in turn, could increase the demand for sex workers. Alternatively the modernization of commercial sex work may create an environment in which the industry is more controlled and less subject to abuses such as trafficking in women for sex work.

Trafficking in Northeast region that recruit women and girls are frequently women in large numbers. Such traffickers in many cases may have been previously trafficked or are currently sex workers. They come in the pretext of domestic servant recruitment drive and mostly they enter into the most poverty stricken ethnic conflict prone areas. They take the women in the pretext of helping them to place in the wealthy family as a domestic servant through the one or two village connection. In Northeast region most domestic recruiters have some link with the other cities Domestic Servant Bureau racket operating in the metros. Most often those recruiters have lived in the cities or travel for work purposes. Some community leaders and jobless youth are also reported to be involved in trafficking in ethnic conflict zone of Northeast region. It is also reported that in many cases relative or family acquaintance of the women and girls who is trafficked, thus there is a potion of trust. This is the most case of domestic servant nexus to trafficking.

Men and women migrate from Northeast region for many purposes to other metros city. The trends of migration has been increasing day by day due to uncertainty of live. Acute poverty, growing adult unemployment adding to the flood and unending ethnic conflict has compelled the many ethnic youth (boys and girls) to migrate in search of better livelihood options in the metros and cities. This ethnic groups are as it is vulnerable in many forms often they faced language barriers, identity crisis from the main stream of the society. In contrary they get exploited in many forms. Women and girls are the most targeted and exploited in many ways including sexual exploitation. It is fact that all migrants are not trafficked. But migration nexus trafficking cases are reported from the North East region. It is impossible to say in number how many of the migrants are trafficked. The context of Northeast vast majority of people who trafficked are migrant workers seeking job and secure lives. They are seeking to escape poverty and unending ethnic conflict, improve their livelihood and send money back home for their near and dear one. They hear about handsome amount of money paid outside through friends and far distance known people or through recruitment agencies, and other individuals who offer them to find them employment and make the travel arrangement. For most trafficked people it is only once they arrive in the place of destination that their real problems begin as the work promised does not exist and they are forced instead to work in jobs or conditions to which they did not agree.

This report therefore seek to highlight at the issue of trafficking within a broader migration framework and to propose policies which who be effective in reducing trafficking and in preventing the human and labour rights violation to which ethnic migrants workers are so often subjected. It also try to focused on the need to recognize about respect the labour and human rights of all migrant workers as set out in the UN Convention on the

Protection of the Rights of All Migrant Workers and Their Families,1990 (subsequent referred to as the 1990 Migrant Convention). It clearly speaks out the need to implement to all the state party to implement the Convention guidelines for the protection of the migrant rights. Most of the trafficked migrants are highly unlikely to reveal what has happened to them when they are initially come into contact with the non-governmental organization. This is for the variety of reasons including, fear of social ostracism, fear of retaliation from traffickers against themselves or families, an unwillingness to discuss what has happened to them because of trauma or shame; a distrust that they will be persecuted. The trafficked person therefore need reflection period.

The Nedan Foundation is a social development organization advocacy and network of concerned individuals, media coalition against trafficking and HIV, Student Union, Human rights activist and CSOs who have joined together with sincere efforts to prevent trafficking of women and children and PLHIV related stigma discrimination in the Northeast region of India. NEDAN has been working in the Northeast region with partners organization called North East Network Forum Against Trafficking & HIV (NENFATH) formed by NEDAN within the eight states of North East Region. Since Northeast region has porous border with South East Asia countries, NEDAN with NENFATH efforts is to combat trans-border trafficking and HIV in the trans-border areas with Northeast Region. There main objectives are

- To unite grass-root CSOs to national level for the social revolution against trafficking & HIV
- To work as pressure groups at different level against trafficking
- To build the capacity of NENFATH partners in countering trans-border trafficking and HIV
- To up-lift the morale of the survivors who are facing social ostracism and helping them to rehabilitate them in their families and society

- To create nation wide campaign amongst the different section of the society to combat trafficking & HIV
- To build positive partnership with neighbouring countries in combating trans-border human trafficking and HIV.

Activities

- NEDAN is working for strengthening positive partnership with neighbouring countries in combating trans-border trafficking and HIV.
- It conducts workshops, consultation and awareness building on human trafficking and HIV
- Provide orientation of girls trafficking and PLHIV stigma discrimination related issues.
- NEDAN is developing a mechanism for collecting, analyzing, disseminating information to the masses on human trafficking and PLHIV issues.
- Advocating and networking with different stakeholders for the policy and its implementation.
- Creating alternative livelihood for rescued from being trafficked and PLHIV families.
- It organizes workshops and seminars in schools and colleges on prevention of trafficking and HIV related issues.

Trafficking of women and children is one of the worst forms of human rights violation. Today it has reached beyond the boundary and jurisdictions. Combating trans-border trafficking & HIV requires joint efforts and concerted action by all the stakeholders from prevention, protection and persecution. Looking into the situation of North East Region (NER) of India having vast porous international borders, Nedan Foundation in collaboration with UNDP RCC, Colombo, Sri-Lanka initiated a dialogue on combating trans-border human trafficking & HIV with Bodoland Territorial Council (BTC) Assam and Royal Kingdom of Bhutan.

Nedan Foundation has substantial experience having worked over a period of time in the trans-border areas and networked with various stakeholders with both the border districts on human trafficking & HIV related stigma and discrimination issues. The two series of Regional Consultations on trans-border human trafficking and HIV have been organized with multisectoral stakeholders from both the border districts areas. Through the series of consultations and dialogue the need for developing a Standard Operating Procedure (SOP) has been recommended with respect to Pre-Rescue, Post Rescue and Repatriation Standard on "Trans- Border Human Trafficking & HIV between Bodoland Territorial Council (BTC) and Royal Kingdom of Bhutan.

The formulation of appropriate Standards/Guidelines is important in order to build positive partnership to carry out the plan of action in a sensitive and professional manner. This SOP is therefore expected to serve as a guideline to address the common concerns with all the stakeholders. This SOP has been developed using the inputs from the regional consultations organised and feedback received from various stakeholders and rescued girls who were trafficked. The existing available journal, reports and related literature have also been reviewed to feed into the preparation of the SOP. The SOP is a first of its kind initiative by a "Civil Society Organisations" to address the transborder human trafficking & HIV through a rights based approach in North East Region with other immediate neighboring country.

There is a general agreement that there is a need to strengthen the capacity of trans-border areas in combating trans-border human trafficking and HIV. South East Asia lay the foundations of a formal pre-rescue, post rescue and repatriation along with providing psychosocial care system in a professional, transparent and accountable manner. One of the starting points of this process is the development and application of routine simple minimum standards for the operation of facilities, in order to ensure that the standard guidelines for the women and children who are survivors of sexual abuse, forced labor, social ostracism and other forms of exploitation are followed uniformly. The guideline presented here presents basic features of standard operating procedure (SOP) and their application to both the neighboring countries' trans-border setting. The standard also discusses the range, purpose, development of standards and guidelines of pre-rescue, post rescue and repatriation of trafficked survivors and reviews existing standards in use throughout. It provides a model of standard operating procedure to be used as a 'guideline tool' by which governments, NGO leaders and workers, trafficking experts, PLHIV, child care experts can use the SOP and apply the standards to protect the survivors through a human right based approach.

The purpose of this SOP is to stimulate a process of discussion and development among governments, NGOs, experts and supporting partners that will lead towards the adoption of uniform minimum standards and guidelines, or 'standard procedure' for both the trans-border areas setting' stakeholders/institutions that work on rescue, repatriation with survivors of sexual abuse and exploitation, specifically survivors of trafficking for sexual purposes and HIV related stigma and discrimination issues. While there is a wide range of standards and guidelines that are applicable to providing standard guidelines for survivors of trafficking and labour exploitation this paper will focus on general 'Operating system' for the operation of facilities with respect to rescue and repatriation care required. Quality of standards in country context can only be developed further by stakeholders of both side taking into account country specific needs and guided by prevailing laws and legal instruments. But the developed SOP as laid down here is expected to facilitate this process through a continuation of collaboration and dialogue and keeping in focus the spirit of the country's Action Plan and SAARC Convention framework.

This Standards and guidelines are applied to many purposes by both the neighboring countries. Some are sets of ethical and practical principles, some are applied to broad-range activities, such as the repatriation and reintegration of trafficked survivors, trafficked and HIV positive women and children and others are applied to specific tasks. There are no hard and fast distinctions between them. For example, specific tasks related to counseling a child trafficked can and should be based on essential principles such as right to confidentiality.

Human rights standards encompass a wide range, from principles and ideological standards applicable to a human situation to specific recommendations for action. Essentially, the UN Convention on the Rights of the Child, CEDAW and the UN Definition on Human trafficking is a set of human rights standards. Some are specifically applied to trafficked persons, such as the document "Human Rights Standards for the Treatment of Trafficked Persons". This provides basic ideological standards to a human situation, include clarifying definitions of terms, and also prescribes specific actions (particularly legal actions) to be taken on the persons' behalf.

Pre-Rescue and Post-Rescue along with Repatriation and Case management standard. These are, as indicated, guidelines on the case management of survivors, including the composition of case management teams, the operation of case conferences, intake, assessment, referral, treatment, reintegration, etc. This is important in the trans-border areas in case of the cases to be follow up in country of origin or the traffickers arrested has the direct linkages with neighboring countries. It is also important in term of HIV positive women and children for access to treatment after the repatriation in the respective country of origin.

Standard repatriation procedures for trafficked survivors and HIV. These are the standards/guidelines with which this paper is concerned. These can include official 'standard Operating guidelines', general guidelines for rescue and repatriation of trafficked survivors and PLHIV, and government regulatory guidelines. Comprehensive 'Standard Operating Procedures' for facilities encompass all, including human rights standards. They contain standards of rights and ethics concerning the treatment of a survivor, specific obligations of a facility regarding the minimum requirements for physical and mental well-being, and guidelines for repatriation and reintegration activities in both destination country and country of origin and international border district areas of both the countries where neighboring countries have open porous borders.

Standards/guidelines for training. These are essential to ensure that the needs of survivors are adequately met by appropriately trained personnel. They include national, international training organization or in-house training standards and competency levels, training assessment guidelines and checklists, and guidelines for the assessment of personnel in handling the survivors. It is also extremely important in term of PLHIV stigma and discrimination in the post rescue time. This standard guideline helps in keeping confidentiality of the PLHIV or trafficked survivors with HIV status after the repatriation of the survivors to country origin.

Standards for the protection of the survivors. The purpose of these are to ensure that the survivor, particularly the women and child, is protected and supported during the process of legal action on her/his behalf, while at the same time ensuring that the necessary legal procedures are correctly undergone to ensure prosecution of the perpetrator. These need standards for legal persons, guidelines for those dealing with the child, and child friendly environment is a must. It is extremely important that the survivor's rights are not violated in the process.

Other specific standards and guidelines include guidelines for family/survivor assessment by social workers, psychologists, etc.; Standard/ guidelines for forensic examination of survivors by physicians; guidelines for the operation of Crisis Intervention Units in international border; guidelines to protect the child against abuse within the facility; guidelines of response to psychological crisis or medical emergency; and others. All are useful and vital, and should complement the 'minimum standards' guidelines for facilities in their protection and support process.

The Salvation Army, a quasi-military church, has come forward to tackle the human trafficking that is silently stalking the Northeast India. The 'India Eastern Territory Anti-Human Trafficking Project', which is part of the Salvation Army's global operation, was today inaugurated at the Aizawl Temple's Booth's conference hall here by state transport minister PC Zoramsangliana. Anti-human trafficking programme was started in Mizoram by the Salvation Army in 2005, and the project launched today was a reinforcement of its ongoing programme. The project is a joint venture of the Salvation Army of the United Kingdom and Mizoram and will cover senstitive areas in the India's Northeast such as Moreh (near Manipur-Myanmar border), Imphal, Churachandpur, Shillong, Guwahati, Siliguri, Fatapukur, Darjeeling, Kalimpong and Namchi.

The areas of operation may be extended as necessary in due course. Raising awareness of human trafficking, and particularly human sex trafficking through the delivery of seminars and presentations to various groups within and outside of The Salvation Army; trainings to take place in social service units that are most likely to come into contact with trafficked persons so that they are able to recognize a trafficked victim and know what to do in this case; developing partnerships with local law enforcement on the issue as well as with other like-minded groups and organizations; developing intentional ministry specific to commercially sexually exploited adults and youths are one of the major modes of operation. The Salvation Army's organ Community Health Action Network (CHAN), which is undertaking the operation, has received a number of cases related to human trafficking. Human trafficking has gone on to become one of the most serious issues plaguing the country in general, and the north-east in particular.

Police and activists have raised an alarm that human traffickers are increasingly turning to India's poor and insurgency-wracked northeastern states in their search for young girls to work in big city brothels. According to sources, more than 300 women and children are trafficked cross border in the state of Meghalaya alone. Over the past five years there has been a rise in reports of missing girls from the remote region of the eight states, an increase which authorities believe is due to trafficking. Police say at least 700 girls from the region have been reported missing over the last five years, 300 of whom disappeared in 2005 alone. But activists estimate thousands of northeastern girls disappear every year - most of whom are not reported by families due to the stigma associated with being part of the sex trade.

Traffickers are mostly women, often well-known in their respective villages, who promise poor, rural families good jobs for their daughters, most of whom are between 12 and 16. But in reality, they sell the girls to brothel owners in towns and cities like New Delhi, Pune, Mumbai and Kolkata, earning between Rs 20,000 - Rs 40,000 for each girl. Police estimate that around 20 percent of the girls in India's big city brothels come from the northeast. At least one million Indian girls and women work in India's sex industry which is estimated to be worth around Rs 400 billion annually, according to the UNODC. The rise in the number of girls disappearing from states like Assam, Meghalaya and Arunachal Pradesh is partly due to tighter surveillance on India's northeastern border with Nepal, where most girls were being trafficked from before.

Authorities say increased security along the border to curb Maoist insurgencies in both countries has deterred many traffickers, and the number of Nepali girls being brought into India annually has halved from around 10,000 three or four years ago. Police, who are more used to fighting rebels in the troubled region, are now receiving training on issues ranging from dealing with traumatised victims to the legal complexities of investigating the crime.

The North-eastern region is an essential part of the nation, and contributes immensely to the process of nation-building. The region has been actively associated with India's freedom movement, socio-cultural development as well as economic growth. Its peoples have distinguished themselves in every walk of life, and its vibrancy and dynamism contributes immensely to India's rich heritage and culture. Therefore, to ensure that each citizen of this region has adequate access to the justice system is a compelling priority for all of us. It is imperative therefore, that we address the needs of this region and pay special attention towards overcoming the impediments that may be endemic to the region, due to its geography, climate or other factors. Local clashes, floods, erosion and other such problems lead to migration and internal displacement, often dividing families. In such unfortunate scenario, women are particularly affected, and are vulnerable to various social evils like trafficking, perpetrated by unscrupulous elements who try to lure these often unsuspecting women with false promises of marriage and employment. Oftentimes, successful rescue and rehabilitation measures have yielded positive results. However, an effective justice mechanism that is able to reach out to one and all will greatly augment all such constructive measures. By affording access to justice system we mean that their valuable rights under the Constitution are safely protected. We hear from the media reports that the public distribution system has been a total failure in the North Eastern region and essential commodities, which are intended to be supplied through such distribution system, are not reaching the common man. Courts and administrators should feel that they have got a greater role to play in ensuring that the poverty alleviation programmes are effectively implemented. Citizens should feel that they are their protectors of their rights.

Some of the major impediments for the access to justice movement, with respect to women in the North East, are illiteracy, lack of awareness, poverty and the like. Almost 35% of the population of the region is below the poverty line, and so, monetary resources are hard to come by. A multi-pronged approach is required to tackle these problems. Firstly, it is necessary to encourage awareness programs that generate academic debate and intellectual deliberation on the most critical issues and result in the creation of constructive and practical ideas that can be implemented for the benefit of the women in the north east. Secondly, sensitization of judicial officers regarding the particular challenges faced by women from the north east is also important, since it would help in ensuring speedy and efficacious justice. Thirdly, a confluence of citizen's forums to promote access to justice would go a long way in promoting public private partnerships and generate societal involvement towards ameliorating the condition of these women. Lastly, the needs of an inclusive society must be addressed and highlighted in order to stimulate developmental work through legal empowerment of communities.

Another matter of serious concern that requires immediate attention is the reports of instances of trafficking of women from Assam and other parts of the north east. It is necessary to note herein that most of these women who are trafficked belong to the poorest strata of society, and, being poor and vulnerable, are often excluded from basic socio-economic services. They suffer the most from natural disasters, become victims of evils like corruption and are thus the most seriously effected part of the entire population. Furthermore, their problems find no vent and relief when the justice system, often the last resort of the downtrodden, leaves them alienated from its doors and they are left frustrated and defenseless against all, in a state of haplessness. Moreover, the absence of an effective and coordinated policy in addressing these issues holistically renders the entire judicial organ incapable of ameliorating the dismal conditions of north-eastern women.

Rising instances of domestic violence also need speedy addressal. An effective use of the law relating to this malpractice will surely lead to its eradication. However, this is possible only through a concerted strategy that addresses instances of physical and mental abuse in a timely manner.

Crimes against women, such as rape and murder, also need to be dealt with a heavy hand by the judiciary. For this, it is necessary for the justice dispensation system to reach out to the grass-root level and remote areas and reduce legal marginalization. The root causes of this marginalization lies in ignorance about basic human rights and fundamental rights. This is further compounded by the problem of illiteracy. Unscrupulous people exploit these illiterates thus depriving the socially and economically marginalized people of access to justice. A sociologically informed approach to reform of legal procedure is needed. Various means may be employed to achieve this. Mobile courts, evening courts and other such projects that have been successfully implemented in many parts of the country may be emulated to reach out to remote areas. Other region-specific strategies may be formulated. This, in addition to awareness programs regarding rights and freedoms of women, would surely yield positive results.

It is heartening to note that the National Legal Services Authority (NALSA) has spearheaded numerous social justice awareness campaigns in various parts of the country, notable among which is the National Legal Literacy Mission. These campaigns will go a long way in the creation of a rights conscious nation and society. Particularly, in the North East, the need of the hour is to increase the number of these awareness campaigns, and take them to the most remote and excluded regions. Only through a concerted attempt in creating legal awareness will we be closer towards building a momentum and a consciousness towards empowering women of the north-east region to enforce their rights effectively. It must, however, be kept in mind that along with such awareness, the judiciary must also be sensitized towards espousing the cause of uplifting and rehabilitating affected women through a rights based approach for the achievement of a just and equitable society.

The present forum is a step towards building a momentum and a consciousness towards the emerging needs of improvement of social justice measures for the most vulnerable and affected groups in the North Eastern Region. While proper implementation of the existing legislations and ensuring punishment to the guilty is to be ensured by the Judiciary, this cannot be done single handedly. It requires the active participation of all organs of the state-the legislature, executive mainly the police force and the judiciary. Nevertheless, the court system plays a central role in guaranteeing access to justice to citizens. Effective access to justice is an important part of any well functioning democracy. India is rightly acclaimed for being an upholder of the rule of law since time immemorial, for achieving a flourishing constitutional order, presided over by an inventive and activist judiciary, aided by a proficient bar, supported by the state and cherished by the public.

In addition, the development of effective alternate dispute redressal forums for the villages and affected groups, improved legal counseling systems and awareness campaigns for the protection of fundamental rights is also necessary. Only through such a synchronized approach can we deliver justice to those who are alienated from it.

NOTES & REFERENCES

1. Interview carried out by *NEDAN*
2. ILO and Community Action centre study on Internal Trafficking among children engaged in prostitution.
3. Sector project against trafficking in women report.
4. The *Telegraph* Newspaper
5. Africa regional report on trafficking in women, forced prostitution and slaverfay - like practices.
6. The *Sentinel* Newspaper
7. *North-east Encyclopedia*
8. The Engkong documentation paper, Assam
9. HNRC study report on Trafficking of Women and Children in India.

5

Prevention and Protection of Trafficking

In the absence of awareness of human rights, the economically and socially deprived people at the grassroots have become easy prey to the trafficking trade. Migrating populations have become most vulnerable to exploitation by traffickers. It's mainly the women, children and poor people from rural area who are the victims of traffickers. Likewise the further impact spoil ones life and pollute the society. The crime of trafficking involves the violation of a whole gamut of laws and human rights. It becomes a threat to society because traffickers operate across borders with impunity, with the growing involvement of organized criminals and generally undermining the rule of law. Trafficking, 'threatens the very fabric of society' because it involves not only criminals but also law enforcers. To address the issue of human trafficking in a holistic and rights based manner. By this I mean a correct and sensitive approach that takes into account several aspects such as right to life; right to security; right to privacy; access to health services; right to self-determination of the trafficked person and addresses the core issue of prevention, protection and prosecution so as to bring about a determined effort to prevent trafficking.

Trafficking of women and children causes untold miseries, as it violates the rights and dignity of the individual in several respects. It amounts to violation of the right to life, right to dignity, right to security, right to privacy, right to health, education, right to self-determination, right to legal remedies and redressal of grievances. More often than not, especially with reference to transborder trafficking, the trafficked victims' right to be heard before decisions are taken on their behalf is also denied. The issue of statelessness' often leads to the denial of the right to return to one's country. From the victimological perspective, the trafficked person is one who suffers several crimes which are perpetrated on her/him.

Despite the oft-reported distortions and problems in justice delivery to the trafficked victims, it is a fact that the state, being held singularly responsible for the welfare of its citizens, has incurred substantial expenditure in addressing the issues related to trafficking. Rescue and rehabilitation programmes and processes cost a lot of money. A case in point is the example of the expenditure incurred by the Department of Women and Child Development (DWCD) in assisting the rescue and rehabilitation programmes of trafficked persons, under the 'grant-in-aid' scheme and the 'SWADHAR' scheme. As on 31st March 2003, DWCD had sanctioned Rs.711.84 lakhs for 3013 beneficiaries under the SWADHAR scheme and Rs.93.94 lakhs for 600 beneficiaries under the 'grant-in-aid' scheme. In fact, during the year 2001-02, the Delhi High Court, while monitoring the rescue and rehabilitation of the trafficked victims, came to know that the police department did not have any funds for the after care of the rescued victims. On the direction of the High Court, the required contingency was provided to the Delhi Police by the DWCD. The cost of post-rescue care and attention will be colossal.

The traffickers inflict damage to the society in several respects which cannot always be measured in tangible terms. It is a fact that continued commercial sexual exploitation leads to severe health hazards like HIV/AIDS not only for the trafficked victim, but also for the 'clientele' and through them, their families. The health hazards are immeasurable. Similarly, the lost dignity of the trafficked victims poses a serious challenge in their reintegration. Most of them are unable to get back to their normal selves. Trafficking causes suffering to the families of the victims in different ways. The damage caused to the children of trafficked victims is untold. By and large, these children are compelled to stay with the trafficked victims in brothels and other exploitative ambience. The growth and development of these children are severely hampered. For want of alternative livelihood options, they too are usually pushed into this exploitative world. The Supreme Court of India had observed (in *Gaurav Jain vs. Union of India*, 1990 Supp SCC 709) that "The children of prostitutes should, however, be not permitted to live in the inferno and the undesirable surroundings of prostitute homes. This was felt particularly so in the case of young girls whose body and mind are likely to be abused with growing age for being admitted into the profession of their mothers". On the whole, the traffickers cause a heavy loss to the society and the damages they inflict are irreparable. Therefore, the best remedy lies in prevention.

Considering the multi-faceted dimensions and the intricate issues involved in trafficking, as well as the continued existence of several types of trafficking throughout history, it may appear almost impossible to prevent trafficking. However, the interesting models developed by several agencies in the country, governmental and non-governmental, have shown that the 'impossible' is only a question of difficulty and of whether appropriate initiatives are taken to surmount the difficulties involved. Case study No. CS-UP-1 explains how intervention by NGOs in partnership with the police, using a 'Rights Promotion Model', has been able to prevent trafficking of several children. In a span of nine months, trafficking of 65 children could be prevented at one transit point. Similarly, case study No. CS-BH-12 explains how a community-based awareness programme has been effectively utilised by the NGO, Bhoruka for preventing trans-border trafficking. This shows that the NGO, in partnership with government agencies, was able to create such an ambience in a known trafficking-prone area, that a stage has come when one can say that these villages have been liberated from the scourge of trafficking. Innumerable police initiatives across the country display ingenious strategies for prevention of trafficking and related crimes. Community policing has been an effective tool in preventing trafficking. These examples not only establish the undeniable fact that trafficking is preventable, but also support the theory that effective prevention is possible only by a functional partnership of governmental and non-governmental agencies.

The UN's Protocol contains a number of provisions aimed

at preventing trafficking. State parties are required to establish policies, programmes and other measures aimed at preventing trafficking and protecting trafficked persons from re-victimization. The existence of vulnerable situations of inequality and injustice coupled with the exploitation of the victim's circumstances by the traffickers and others cause untold harm to the trafficked victim who faces a multiplicity of rights violations. Therefore policies, programmes and strategies that address prevention have to be unique with a focus on and an orientation towards all these issues. Accordingly the prevention of trafficking needs to be addressed not only in relation to the source areas but also in the demand areas the transit points and the trafficking routes. Strategies in all these areas have to be oriented towards the specific characteristics of the situation and the target groups.

- The best method of prevention is its integration it with prosecution and protection. Prosecution includes several tasks like the identification of the traffickers bringing them to the book, confiscating their illegal assets. Protection of the trafficked victim includes all steps towards the redressal of their grievances thus helping the victim survive, rehabilitate and establish herself/himself. Thus prosecution and protection contribute to prevention.
- The strategies should address the issues of livelihood options and opportunities by focusing on efforts to eradicate poverty, illiteracy etc. There should be special packages for women and children in those communities where entry into CSE may be perceived as the only available option. Education and other services should be oriented towards capacity building and the consequent empowerment of vulnerable groups.
- Gender discrimination and patriarchal mindset are important constituents and catalysts of the vulnerability of women and girl children. This manifests itself in several serious violations of women's rights such as high incidence of female foeticide and infanticide and the discrimination against women in healthcare, education and employment. Since these are vulnerability factors

that trigger trafficking prevention strategies need to be oriented accordingly.

- Natural calamities and manmade disturbances do exacerbate the vulnerability situation. Therefore relief and aftercare programmes need to have specific components focused on the rights of women and children.
- At the micro level the prevention of trafficking in the source areas requires a working partnership between the police and NGOs. Public awareness campaigns and community participation are key to prevention programmes. Prevention is best achieved by community policing.
- Political will is an essential requirement to combat trafficking.
- Creating legal awareness is one of the most important functions of any social action programme because without legal awareness it is not possible to promote any real social activism. Legal awareness empowers people by making them aware of their rights, and can work towards strengthening them to develop zero tolerance towards abuse and exploitation.
- Immigration officials at the borders need to be sensitized so that they can network with the police as well as with NGOs working on preventing trafficking.
- Help lines and help booths are very important for providing timely help to any person in distress. The Ministry of Social Justice and Empowerment is considering collaboration between government agencies and NGOs for setting up help lines and help booths that can provide timely assistance to child victims. It will be appropriate if the Child lines all over India, NGOs working on child rights, missing person bureaus and police help lines are linked together as a formidable tool against trafficking.

Once rescued, the victims are often sent to rescue homes.

The field research shows that in many places, the police is reluctant to carry out rescue operations because of the lack of rescue homes. This is an aggravating factor perpetuating trafficking. There is a genuine need for an adequate number of proper Homes, where post-rescue care and attention can be given to the rescued victims. This will help in prevention of re-trafficking also. These Homes should have adequate infrastructure and human resources to counsel the rescued victim, detraumatise her and empower her. Proper knowledge and skill-based training should be provided, keeping the best interests of the victim in mind. These training programmes should not only empower her economically and socially but also make her aware of her legal rights and redressal mechanisms.

The children of women who are subjected to commercial sexual exploitation are highly vulnerable and liable to be trafficked at any time. Therefore, preventing trafficking of these highly vulnerable children requires their rescue without any delay. In such situations, effective intelligence, followed by prompt law-enforcement, can prevent trafficking. Vulnerable persons who are on the threshold of exploitation need to be rescued, sequestered and conscientised, studied psychiatrically and given personalised protection. Pre-emptive semi-custody, with facilities for economic self-reliance and moral normalisation, are essential to prevent trafficking of such persons. "Prevention is better than cure and so, pre-emptive quasi-detention is a therapeutic necessity, if the social objective of ITPA is to succeed," says Justice V.R. Krishna Iyer.[1]

The best interests of the woman/child should be the crucial factor in deciding the fate of the rescued persons. In one instance, releasing rescued minor girls to their advocate in Mumbai has resulted in their being re-trafficked (refer case study No. CS-MH-1). Therefore, the authorities who sit in judgment about the future of the rescued person should keep in mind the best interests of the child. Proper 'home verification' can reveal the situation at home. Effective counselling can help the trafficked person to decide for herself as to what would be the best course of action for her. This approach would prevent her from being retrafficked.

Sometimes, the brothel owners, pimps or traffickers come in the guise of the victims' parents or relatives. They bail them out from the courts/rescue homes, etc., only to re-traffic them. Therefore, proper identification of parents/relatives needs to be done before releasing trafficked victims.

More often than not, trans-border trafficking takes place due to poor law-enforcement on the borders and absence of effective partnership between NGOs and law-enforcement agencies across the border. The case study of the Bangladesh National Women Lawyers' Association (BNWLA) is an example of effective police-NGO partnership in preventing trafficking (refer case study No. CS-BD-1). Similarly, the case study by an NGO, Maiti Nepal, also presents the justification for an effective partnership between the police and NGOs, extending beyond borders, for preventing trafficking (refer case study No. CS-NP-3). As this is a transnational issue, it has to be appropriately dealt with. The Ministries of Home Affairs and External Affairs have to join hands to establish this kind of network. The agencies working on the borders, viz. BSF, SSB, etc., need to have close working partnerships with NGOs, especially those who have effective networking with NGOs across the border.

Prevention programmes and strategies should also be specially oriented to the demand areas, the transit points and the destinations. There is no doubt that trafficking is demand-driven The greater the demand for trafficked victims, the greater will be the magnitude of trafficking. The case study of Goa (vide case study No. CS-GA-1), explaining the shifting of the source areas supplying trafficked victims to the Baina red-light area, is a reference point. This case study has shown that even when the supply areas in Karnataka 'dried up', the demand in Goa did not reduce and that the continued demands, and probably the increased demands, 'created' other source areas. Therefore, the supply areas shifted from Karnataka to Andhra Pradesh. This case study explains the importance of addressing the demand factor for preventing trafficking. The programmes and strategies of addressing the demand areas should be oriented to the trends and patterns in demand as well as the perceptions of the clientele.

Effective law-enforcement in punishing the clients, who are abettors and accomplices in the organized crime of trafficking, especially with reference to child trafficking and child sexual abuse, will have a detrimental effect. Similarly, bringing to book the traffickers, the pimps, the brothel keepers and other exploitators who operate in the demand area is also an important aspect of prevention of trafficking. Prevention strategies at the demand areas have to be not only reactive, but also proactive. Public campaigns and targeted interventions to educate the universe of clientele on health issues and rights issues can make a marked difference. As the study revealed, a substantial segment of the clientele comprises adolescents, mostly misdirected youth, visiting brothels out of curiosity or adventurism. Such people need to be counselled, socialised and oriented to women's rights, child rights, health issues and related matters.

Prevention strategies need to be addressed along the trafficking routes and at the transit points also. Intervention at these places, where trafficking becomes more or less visible, can be an effective tool to prevent trafficking, before the trafficked person is exploited. The Rights Intervention Cells started by SEWA at Sanauli, Gorakhpur and Bahraich, involving NGO workers and police officials, have demonstrated their effective role in preventing crime. The Sanuali experiment (refer case study No. CS-UP-1) shows that over a period of nine months, they were able to prevent trafficking of 65 girls. But for this intervention, these girls would have ended up as victims of CSE in some brothels in India. This experiment by SEWA in Sanauli is a classic example of community policing in preventing trafficking.

Integrated model of development and welfare: Integrating the anti-trafficking component with other programmes, projects and policies, especially those of the Departments of Home, Criminal Justice, Social Justice, Labour, Women and Child Development, etc. can make a tremendous impact in the economic and social empowerment of the vulnerable persons and, thereby, prevent trafficking.

The media has a large role to play in preventing trafficking. Case study No. CS-NE-6 explains how the media-NGO interface worked as a powerful tool in generating public awareness against trafficking. The media can make the public aware of their rights and, thereby, generate and augment human potential against exploitation. It can promote various government schemes addressing the vulnerability factors. The media can also facilitate the working of NGOs by creating public opinion in favour of them and, thereby, making their programmes broad-based. At the same time, the media also has to keep in mind the provisions of law that protect the victims' exploitation. Section 21 of the Juvenile Justice Act prohibits the publication of name, etc. of a juvenile involved in any proceeding under the Act. Section 228A IPC prohibits the disclosure of identity of a victim of rape and certain other offences. Keeping in view these legal provisions and the rights of the victims, the media can play a powerful role in preventing trafficking.

Accountability: Fixing accountability of the government officials, whose duty it is to ensure prevention of crime, is another aspect that needs to be stressed. On the one hand, this requires appropriate and timely action against negligent officials to hold them accountable for their omissions and commissions. On the other hand, accountability could be utilised as a positive tool in improving the morale and efficiency of the officials concerned, especially by promoting, facilitating, advertising and rewarding the good work done by anybody in combating and preventing trafficking.

Most of the trafficking-prevention initiatives of NGOs as well as the government have suffered for want of funds. Case study No. CS-DL-29 shows that the service centre started by JWP, Delhi, for the children of victims of CSE, despite being an effective experiment in preventing trafficking, has had to deal with serious financial constraints. Involvement of corporates and business houses is an essential requirement. The best alliance against trafficking is a partnership of government agencies (GO) with non-governmental organisations (NGOs) and Corporate Houses (CORPS). This integration of 'GONGO CORPS' can make a tremendous impact on trafficking, as substantiated by case study No. CS-DL-30. Government departments and agencies need to coordinate their activities. The water-tight compartmentalisation of policies, programmes and projects has to be done away with. Similarly, governmental agencies have to recognise the role of NGOs and ensure effective partnership. Case studies on community policing illustrate the fact that such a partnership is the best strategy in any given situation. The Thailand experience in anti-trafficking can be considered to be a good model. They have MOUs between the related government agencies, among NGOs and between the government and NGOs. The networking of NGOs with the government has already been envisaged in the ITPA, where there is a provision for constituting an Advisory Body of NGOs. This has more strength than an MOU as the former has legal sanction.

Involving local leaders: Case studies on the involvement of panchayati raj institutions (PRIs) in Tamil Nadu and West Bengal have shown how the participation of the local elected leaders can make a marked difference in preventing trafficking. The village-level and district level committees involving the officials in the district administration, district police and elected representatives of PRIs have the potential to be a formidable force at the ground level in not only creating awareness and initiating preventive strategies but also as a strong contingent acting against traffickers. There lies a huge potential in empowering the panchayat bodies elsewhere in the country and involving them in the process of counter-trafficking.

Legal literacy: "Creating legal awareness is one of the most important functions of any Social Action Programme because without legal awareness it is not possible to promote any real social activism," says Justice P.N. Bhagwati.[2] The case study by an NGO in Nepal (case study No. CS-NP-1) has shown how legal awareness can be an effective tool for creating an anti-trafficking movement. Legal awareness empowers people by making them aware of their rights and, therefore, works towards strengthening them to develop zero tolerance to abuse and exploitation.

The lack of coordination in addressing the issues involved in trafficking across the country has been a serious impediment to the prevention of trafficking. Several children rescued from brothels in Mumbai, who were to be rehabilitated in their communities in the North-East, were languishing in rescue homes in Mumbai because of the delay in 'home verification'. Things started moving only when an NGO took the initiative. There is an urgent need for a national coordinating mechanism to deal with all aspects of trafficking, with specific focus on prevention. This could be set up as a National Nodal Agency against trafficking, which should be able to coordinate the activities of various departments and agencies, both governmental as well as NGOs, CBOs, etc.

Immigration officials at the borders need to be sensitised so that they can network with the police as well as NGOs working on prevention of trafficking.

There is a linkage between missing persons and trafficking, as several case studies have shown. The chapter on Missing Persons has established the importance of addressing this linkage as an effective tool to prevent trafficking.

Helplines and help booths are very important requirements for providing timely help to any person in distress. Case study No. CS-BH-20 shows how Childline, Patna has been instrumental in preventing several children from being exploited. The Ministry of Social Justice and Empowerment is considering a collaboration between governmental agencies and NGOs in setting up helplines and help booths to provide timely assistance to child victims. It will be appropriate if the Childlines all over India, NGOs working on child rights, missing persons bureaus and police helplines are linked together, so that it can become a formidable tool in preventing trafficking.

Proper law-enforcement is essential for prevention of trafficking. This requires a multidimensional approach. The data collected from police officials shows that only 40 per cent of trafficking crimes are reported and 60 per cent crimes go unreported. Similarly, despite the fact that the majority of the exploiters are males, among the arrested persons, 92.9 per cent were females and only 7.1 per cent were males. The concomitant figures of prosecution and conviction of females, who are usually the victims, and their consequent re-trafficking, has been brought out in the data obtained from the police. Therefore, prevention of trafficking calls for a radical change in the existing paradigm of law-enforcement.

Indian missions abroad, especially in those countries which are either source areas or demand areas, need to network with the concerned agencies in order to make a strong impact in the prevention of trafficking. They have a large role to play in arresting sex tourism. Case study No. CS-MH-12, which deals with a convicted paedophile, explains how several foreign nationals were regularly indulging in paedophiliac activities with impunity for a long time. One of the paedophiles, who managed to escape from India, was later put on the 'look out notice'. He was apprehended by alert immigration officials in India, despite the fact that he was travelling in disguise, under a different name and passport. This calls for proper verification and monitoring of such persons while granting visa, in order to ensure that paedophiles are not allowed entry.

The SAARC Convention requires several initiatives to be taken for prevention of trafficking. One of them is setting up a joint task force. At present, the District Magistrates and the Superintendents of Police of several districts bordering Nepal, on their own, have informal arrangements with their counterparts across the border to deal with this problem. There is a need to strengthen these initiatives and develop them into institutionalised mechanisms to prevent trafficking.

The SAARC Convention, under Article VIII, identifies several measures to prevent trafficking in women and children. In addition to the regional task force mentioned above, the measures suggested by the SAARC Convention include: (a) Training and assistance to the concerned authorities for effective investigation and prosecution, (b) Sensitising law-enforcement agencies and the judiciary, (c) Setting up of bilateral mechanisms, (d) Regular exchange of information in respect of agencies, institutions and individuals involved in trafficking, identifying the *modus operandi* and the routes used by the traffickers. Sharing of information, including fingerprints, photographs, police records, conviction records and methods of operation of those involved in trafficking, (e) Initiating necessary measures within the countries for supervising the employment agencies to prevent trafficking under the guise of recruitment, (f) Focussed prevention and development efforts in the source areas of trafficking, and (g) Promoting awareness through media and other channels on the problems and causes of trafficking.

The responses across the world to prevent trafficking are many. For example, the Victims of Trafficking and Violations Protection Act 2000 (VTVPA) of the United States provides its government with a mandate to address the issue of trafficking across the world. The prevention strategy of VTVPA includes (a) economic assistance, (b) training, (c) police protection and (d) detection and investigation. The Act also provides financial assistance and technical support for prevention strategies in other countries.

In India, there are several initiatives by the Government of India and the state governments. The National Plan of Action by the DWCD has provision for elaborate steps to prevent trafficking. The Indian Constitution is probably unique in that it specifically addresses the issue of trafficking of human beings (Article 23). The focus on prevention of trafficking under the ITPA shows a paradigm shift from the earlier Act, i.e. Suppression of Immoral Trafficking Act (SITA). Accordingly, the government has launched the National Plan of Action as well as several initiatives and programmes. Long-term training cum income generation programmes have been launched by the government in several states. (For details, the chapter on government response may be seen.) Efforts are afoot to make amendments in the existing legislation. There is a need to have a separate chapter on prevention in this statute. (For details, see the discussion in the chapter on changes in the law.)

Joint initiative by UN bodies: The JIT has been instrumental in setting up a joint front of officials and activists across the Indo-Nepal border. Such ad hoc arrangements can be strengthened and institutionalized by ratification by the governments concerned. Moreover, the members of the joint front can be empowered by providing them with adequate resources and other capacity building programmes like regular training.

Similarly, the commendable initiatives of several NGOs across the country in preventing trafficking can be developed as models, which need to be strengthened, propagated and facilitated. The details of the same may be seen in the chapter on community response.

Attitudinal orientation: Research has shown that trafficking is an issue of low priority for law-enforcement agencies. Similarly, among the NGOs, there are very few which are genuinely committed to prevention of trafficking. International attention to trafficking and the involvement of several funding agencies have created a favourable situation for several NGOs to work in the field. Since trafficked victims are subjected to the worst forms of human rights violations, it is imperative that prevention is considered to be the best remedy. This calls for an appropriate attitudinal orientation among the governmental and nongovernmental agencies.

The Indian Penal Code (IPC) enacted in 1860 has several provisions, which try to protect girls/women against forced illicit sexual intercourse. The following are the sections related to trafficking in the Indian Penal Code:

- 363 A – Kidnapping or maiming minor for purposes of begging Kidnapping or abducting with intent secretly and wrongfully to confine a person
- 366 - Kidnapping, abducting or inducing woman to compel her marriage.
- 366A - Procuration of a minor girl
- 366B - Importation of girl from foreign country
- 370 - Buying or disposing of any person as slave
- 372 - Selling minor for purposes of prostitution
- 373 - Buying minor for purposes of prostitution
- 376 - Punishment for rape

The main act, deals with the phenomenon of prostitution, is Prevention of Immoral Traffic Act (ITPA) 1996, the amended version of the earlier Act, Suppression of Immoral Traffic in Girls and women, which was enacted in 1956. The Suppression of Immoral Traffic in Women and Girls Act of 1956 addressed street prostitution but not brothels. The Act was amended in 1996 and renamed as the Immoral Traffic in Persons Prevention Act. It addresses prostitution of minors (16-18 years of age) and children (below 16 years).[3]

Some of the important sections under the Immoral Traffic Prevention Act, 1986 (ITPA)

Section 2(f): Prostitution - Sexual exploitation or abuse of persons for commercial purpose

Section 2(h): Public Place – any place intended for use by or accessible to the public and includes any public conveyance

Section 2(aa): Child means a person who has not completed 16 years

Section 2(cb): Minor means a person between 16 – 18 years of age

Section 13(4): The Central Government may, for the purpose of investigating any offence under this Act or under any other law for the time being in force.

In 1949 (articles 1 & 2 of the 1949 Convention for the Suppression on the Traffic in Persons and of the Exploitation of the Prostitution of Others), the concept of trafficking has been extended to include trafficking for the purpose of other forms of exploitation, which also includes forced marriages and forced labour, but the debates on human trafficking have primarily focused on sexual exploitation as a main purpose for trafficking, excluding discussions on labour issues.

The Juvenile Justice (Care and Protection of Children) Act, 2000:

Some relevant sections:

- Section 2 (k): "juvenile" or "child" means a person who has completed eighteen years of age.

- Section 2 (d): "Child in need of care and protection" means a child Who has a parent or guardian and such parent or guardian is unfit or incapacitated to exercise control over the child, Who is being or is likely to be grossly abused, tortured or exploited for the purpose of sexual abuse and illegal acts, Who is found vulnerable and is likely to be induced not drug abuse or trafficking, Who is likely to be abused for unconscionable gains.

Under this act, the State Governments have been empowered to constitute for every district or groups of districts one or more Child Welfare Committees (section 29) for exercising the powers and discharge of duties in relation to child in need of care and protection under the Act. The committee shall have final authority to dispose of cases for the care, protection, treatment, development, and rehabilitation of the children and as well as to provide for their basic needs and protection of human rights.

It is evident from the above that there is no existing law that deals with trafficking for labour purposes and thus the issue has been addressed either under the preview of The Child Labour (Prohibition and Regulation) Act of 1986 or under the Bonded Labour (System) Abolition Act, 1976.

What makes it difficult to address the phenomenon is also the uniformity in the age of the child in all concerned acts:

- The Factories Act, 1948 and the Child Labour (Prohibition and Regulation) Act, 1986; under which a child is a person below the age of 14 years.
- The Indian Penal Code, 1960 under which the definition of a child is a person below 12 years of age.
- The Juvenile Justice Act, 1986; under which a child is a person below 16 years of age for a male child and below 18 years of age for a female child.
- The Child Marriage Restraint Act, 1992; under which a child is a person below the age of 21 in case of male and below the age of 18 in case of females.

- The Immoral Traffic Prevention Acts, 1996, says a female child should not exceed 16 years of ages, while a minor is defined as being up to 18 years old.

These discrepancies in law provide ample room for perpetrators to escape from the hands of law. These laws need to be amended to conform to the International Convention on the Rights of the Child, which defines child as not exceeding 18 years of age.

Indian government authorities made significant progress in law enforcement efforts against sex trafficking and forced child labor during the year, but made little progress in addressing bonded labor. The government prohibits some forms of trafficking for commercial sexual exploitation through the Immoral Trafficking Prevention Act (ITPA). Prescribed penalties under the ITPA, ranging from seven years' to life imprisonment, are sufficiently stringent and commensurate with those prescribed for other grave crimes, such as rape. India also prohibits bonded and forced labor through the Bonded Labour (Abolition) Act of 1976, the Child Labour (Prohibition and Regulation) Act of 1986, and the Juvenile Justice Act of 1986. These laws were ineffectively enforced, and their prescribed penalties—a maximum of three years in prison—are not sufficiently stringent. Indian authorities also use Sections 366(A) and 372 of the Indian Penal Code, prohibiting kidnapping and selling minors into prostitution, respectively, to arrest traffickers. Penalties prescribed under these provisions are a maximum of ten years' imprisonment and a fine. Although Section 8 of the ITPA allows the arrest of trafficked women for soliciting, the Indian cabinet debated for another year proposed amendments that would give trafficking victims greater protections.

State governments continued to demonstrate efforts to address forced child labor, but failed to punish most traffickers. During the year, the New Delhi government rescued more than 100 -children from forced labor situations, such as the February 2009 rescue of 35 children found enslaved in four small factories making leather products under hazardous and forced conditions without pay. In Jharkhand (with a population of 29 million people), the state labor ministry and police, in collaboration with an NGO, conducted raids on 120 establishments during a planned operation and rescued 208 children from forced or bonded labor situations.

The central government and state governments continued to demonstrate efforts to combat sex trafficking of women and children, though convictions and punishments of sex traffickers were infrequent. The central government's National Crime Records Bureau provided limited comprehensive data, compiled from state and union territory governments, on actions taken against sex trafficking offenses in 2007. The 2007 data indicated that 4,087 cases were registered (investigations started) which likely includes sex trafficking cases referred to courts for prosecution as well as cases investigated and closed without such referrals. This data did not include reported prosecutions and convictions. Data for 2008 will not be available until 2010.

In Andhra Pradesh, Bihar, Maharashtra, Goa, and West Bengal (with a combined population of 360 million people), government officials registered 964 sex trafficking cases, conducted 379 rescue operations, helped rescue 1,653 victims, arrested 1,970 traffickers (including 856 customers), convicted 30 sex traffickers, helped rehabilitate 876 sex trafficking victims, and trained 13,490 police officers and prosecutors. In Mumbai, authorities prosecuted 10 sex trafficking cases but obtained no convictions in 2008. In Andhra Pradesh, courts convicted and sentenced eleven traffickers to imprisonment for 10 to 14 years. Tamil Nadu's state government reported arrests of 1,097 sex trafficking offenders in 2008, though the number of trafficking prosecutions and convictions during the reporting period was not reported. The city of Pune attained its first sex trafficking conviction in 2008.

During the reporting period, the central government made little progress to investigate, prosecute, convict, and punish labor trafficking offenders. However, it allocated $18 million to the Ministry of Home Affairs to create 297 anti-human trafficking units across the nation to train and sensitize law enforcement officials. According to NGOs, state-level officials who received such training in the past are increasingly recognizing women in prostitution as potential victims of trafficking and therefore not arresting them for solicitation. In Tamil Nadu (with a population of 65 million people), an NGO reported a significant improvement in how police file charges in bonded labor cases. The police now also employ the Indian Penal Code's tougher provisions, which allow bonded labor cases to be processed more quickly through the judicial system.

The significant problem of public officials' complicity in sex trafficking and forced labor remained largely unaddressed by central and state governments during the reporting period. Corrupt law enforcement officers reportedly continued to facilitate the movement of sex trafficking victims, protect brothels that exploit victims, and protect traffickers and brothel keepers from arrest and other threats of enforcement. India reported no prosecutions, convictions, or sentences of government officials for trafficking-related offenses during the reporting period.

India's efforts to protect victims of trafficking varied from state to state. Protection efforts often suffered from a lack of sufficient financial and technical support from government sources, and protection for victims of labor trafficking remained very weak. Under its Swadhar program - which covers a broad range of activities of which anti-sex trafficking is one — the government supports over 200 shelters with an annual budget of more than $1 million to provide care for more than 13,000 women and girls rescued from a range of difficult circumstances, including sex trafficking. The Ministry of Women and Child Development continued to give grants under its Ujjawala program for the prevention, rescue, rehabilitation, and reintegration of sex trafficking victims. The ministry approved funding for at least 53 state projects under this program, benefiting more than 1,700 victims. Since August 2008, the ministry provided the states of Karnataka, Maharashtra, Manipur, and Nagaland almost $243,000 for 18 projects at 12 rehabilitation centers. Andhra Pradesh established a fund specifically for victim rehabilitation, giving victims rescued from sexual exploitation $200 in temporary relief. Tamil Nadu began providing free legal aid and drug and alcohol addiction counseling services in state shelters to trafficking victims. The Delhi government established a helpline staffed by NGOs in February 2009 to help rescue children found begging.

Although victims of bonded labor are entitled to 20,000 rupees ($400) from the government if they are certified as victims of bonded labor and may be housed in government shelters, disbursement of rehabilitation funds is sporadic and the quality of care in many shelters is not high. NGOs reported that some corrupt local officials take unlawful "commissions" from the rehabilitation packages. Overall, government authorities do not proactively identify and rescue bonded laborers, so few victims receive assistance, though Tamil Nadu showed the greatest effort to identify and assist victims of bonded labor. In other states, NGOs provided the bulk of protection services to bonded labor victims.

The central government's Ministry of Overseas Indian Affairs, during the reporting period, showed resolve to address the trafficking of Indian migrant workers. For example, in September 2008, the Government ordered an inquiry after reports surfaced of girls from northeastern India being trafficked to Malaysia for sex work. The Government arrested the travel agent, promptly rescued the girls and paid for their repatriation to India. The Ministry also drafted an amendment to the Emigration Act that would increase administrative penalties for Indian labor recruitment agencies involved in fraudulent recruitment or human trafficking. Some Indian diplomatic missions in destination countries, especially those in the Middle East, provide significant services, including temporary shelters to nationals who have been trafficked. Some foreign victims trafficked to India are not subject to removal. Those who are subject to removal are not offered legal alternatives to their removal to countries where they may face hardship or retribution. NGOs reported in the past some Bangladesh victims of sex trafficking were pushed back across the border without protection services. During the reporting period, India worked closely with Bangladesh on resolving cross-border trafficking issues, including formally designating a government official to handle such issues during Home Secretary-level discussions in August 2008.

Government shelters for sex trafficking victims are found in all major cities, but the quality of care varies widely. In

Maharashtra, West Bengal, Tamil Nadu, and Andhra Pradesh, state authorities operated homes for minor victims of sex trafficking. Although states have made some improvements to their shelter care, victims in these facilities do not receive comprehensive protection services, such as psychological assistance from trained counselors. Many victims decline to testify against their traffickers due to fear of retribution by traffickers and India's sluggish and overburdened judicial system. The government does not actively encourage victims to participate in cases against their traffickers.

India continued to conduct information and education campaigns against trafficking in persons and child labor. In late 2008 the central government completed its 18-month long consultation process with government and NGO stakeholders on a comprehensive "Integrated Plan of Action to Prevent and Combat Human Trafficking with Special Focus on Children and Women." Overall, the government's anti-trafficking policies and programs remained framed by the limited perspective of human trafficking defined as the trafficking of women and children for sexual exploitation, in line with the 2002 South Asian Association for Regional Cooperation Convention on Combating Trafficking of Women and Children for Prostitution. Kerala (with a population of 33 million people and India's largest source of laborers who migrate overseas regularized recruitment agencies and introduced a toll free number for potential migrants. In January 2009, the central government approved a nationwide model that merges its national educational and poverty alleviation programs together to combat child labor.

While the government made modest efforts to prevent trafficking for commercial sexual exploitation, it did not report new or significant efforts to prevent the large problem of bonded labor. The Ministry of Women and Child Development remained the central government's coordinator of anti-trafficking policies and programs, though its ability to enhance interagency coordination and accelerate anti-trafficking efforts across the bureaucracy remained weak. In August 2008, a UN report alleged several Indian peacekeepers posted in the Democratic Republic of the Congo had been involved in paying minor Congolese girls for sex in 2007 and 2008. In March 2009, the Indian military exonerated the soldiers after conducting an investigation. According to a Government of India official, training for Indian soldiers deployed in peacekeeping missions includes awareness about trafficking. In May 2008, the Ministry of Women and Child Development created a think-tank to expand public-private partnerships to play a greater role in preventing and combating human trafficking.

The Ministry of Labour and Employment issued a "Protocol on Prevention, Rescue, Repatriation, and Rehabilitation of Trafficked and Migrant Child Labor" in May 2008 to guide state and district level authorities and NGOs, and expanded the central governments list of occupations that are banned from employing children. The government undertook several measures to reduce demand for commercial sex acts during the reporting period, such as the arrests of 856 customers of prostitutions in Andhra Pradesh, Maharastra, Bihar, Goa and West Bengal. India has not ratified the 2000 UN TIP protocol.

The Constitution of India, the fundamental law of the land, forbids trafficking in persons. The commitment to address the problem of trafficking in human beings is also reflected in various laws/legislations and policy documents of the Government of India. The Indian Penal Code, 1860 contains more than 20 provisions that are relevant to trafficking and impose criminal penalties for offences like kidnapping, abduction, buying or selling a person for slavery/labour, buying or selling a minor for prostitution, importing/procuring a minor girl, rape, etc.[4]

The Immoral Traffic (Prevention) Act, 1956 (ITPA), initially enacted as the 'Suppression of Immoral Traffic in Women and Girls Act, 1956, is the main legislative tool for preventing and combating trafficking in human beings in India. However, till date, its prime objective has been to inhibit/abolish traffic in women and girls for the purpose of prostitution as an organized means of living. The Act criminalizes the procurers, traffickers and profiteers of the trade but in no way does it define 'trafficking' *per se* in human beings. Hence there is a marked absence of any standard guideline for intervention or law enforcement in preventing trafficking from occurring. The Government is in the process of amending the ITPA, with a view to making the laws victim-friendly and, at the same time, making punishment for traffickers more stringent and putting greater criminal culpability on them. India has not ratified the 2000 UN TIP Protocol. Also there is a UN Convention against Transnational Organised Crime (the Palermo Protocol) that will, when implemented, give a comprehensive definition of trafficking, but this has still not been ratified.

However, the other relevant Acts which address the issue of trafficking in India are the Karnataka *Devdasi* (Prohibition of Dedication) Act, 1982; Child Labour (Prohibition and Regulation) Act, 1986; Andhra Pradesh *Devdasi* (Prohibiting Dedication) Act, 1989; Information Technology Act, 2000; the Goa Children's Act, 2003; and the Juvenile Justice (Care and Protection of Children) Amendment Act, 2006. Beside these, there are also certain other collateral laws having relevance to trafficking. These are the Indian Evidence Act, 1872; Child Marriage Restraint Act, 1929; Young Persons (Harmful Publications) Act, 1956; Probation of Offenders Act, 1958; Criminal Procedure Code, 1973; Bonded Labour System (Abolition) Act, 1976; Indecent Representation of Women (Prohibition) Act, 1986; and the Transplantation of Human Organs Act, 1994.[5]

India continues to conduct information and education campaigns against trafficking in persons and child labor. In late 2008 the central government completed its 18-month long consultation process with the Ministry of Women and Child Development, Ministry of Home Affairs, National Human Rights Commission and National Commission for Women have decided to work in unison and draw up an Integrated Plan of Action to Prevent and Combat Human Trafficking with Special Focus on Children and Women. In January 2009, the central government approved a nationwide model that merges its national educational and poverty alleviation programs together to combat child labor. The government undertook several measures to reduce demand for commercial sex acts during the reporting period, such as the arrests of 856 customers of prostitution in Andhra Pradesh, Maharashtra, Bihar, Goa, and West Bengal.

India's efforts to protect victims of trafficking varied from state to state. Protection efforts often suffered from a lack of sufficient financial and technical support from government sources, and protection for victims of labor trafficking remained very weak. Under its Swadhar program, which covers a broad range of activities of which anti-sex trafficking is one, the government supports over 200 shelters with an annual budget of more than $1 million to provide care for more than 13,000 women and girls rescued from a range of difficult circumstances, including sex trafficking. The Ministry of Women and Child Development continues to give grants under its Ujjawala program for the prevention, rescue, rehabilitation, and reintegration of sex trafficking victims. The ministry approved funding for at least 53 state projects under this program, benefiting more than 1,700 victims. Since August 2008, the ministry provided the states of Karnataka, Maharashtra, Manipur, and Nagaland almost $243,000 for 18 projects at 12 rehabilitation centers. Andhra Pradesh established a fund specifically for victim rehabilitation, giving victims rescued from sexual exploitation $200 in temporary relief. Tamil Nadu began providing free legal aid and drug and alcohol addiction counseling services in state shelters to trafficking victims. The Delhi government established a helpline staffed by NGOs in February 2009 to help rescue children found begging.

Government shelters for sex trafficking victims are found in all major cities, but the quality of care varies widely. In Maharashtra, West Bengal, Tamil Nadu, and Andhra Pradesh, state authorities operated homes for minor victims of sex trafficking. Although states have made some improvements to their shelter care, victims in these facilities do not receive comprehensive protection services, such as psychological assistance from trained counselors. Many victims decline to testify against their traffickers due to fear of retribution by traffickers and India's sluggish and overburdened judicial system. The government does not actively encourage victims to participate in cases against their traffickers.

Indian government authorities made significant progress in law enforcement efforts against sex trafficking and forced child labor during the year, but made little progress in addressing bonded labor. The Constitution of India, under Article 23, prohibits trafficking of human beings for any exploitation. However, the ITPA takes into consideration only trafficking for sexual exploitation. This is a special legislation with stringent provisions for punishing violators and exploiters, with enhanced punishment for sexual exploitation of children. There are several steps prescribed in this legislation towards prevention of trafficking. However, it is a fact that most of the provisions of the law remain un-enforced and unimplemented. Usually, there are serious distortions in implementation. Despite ITPA being a social legislation, no role has so far been envisaged for DWCD in monitoring the law enforcement process.

State governments continued to demonstrate efforts to address forced child labor, but failed to punish most traffickers. In February 2009, the New Delhi government rescued over 100 children from forced labor situations. In Jharkhand (with a population of 29 million people), the state labor ministry and police, in collaboration with an NGO, conducted raids on 120 establishments during a planned operation and rescued 208 children from forced or bonded labor situations. The central government has allocated $18 million to the Ministry of Home Affairs to create 297 anti-human trafficking units across the nation to train and sensitize law enforcement officials. According to NGOs, state-level officials who received such training in the past are increasingly recognizing women in prostitution as potential victims of trafficking and therefore not arresting them for solicitation.

Church of North India (CNI) has intervened in combating human trafficking in the eastern Himalayan area where the closure of tea gardens has made the children and women vulnerable to trafficking. CNI has an intensive base with the community in source areas and has been able to intervene through CNI's resource pool of institutes, organizations and community based groups by integration of awareness on trafficking in the existing programmes.

The Church also makes use of its local resources in terms of women, youth and pastors to reach out to the larger community and also involves different stakeholders such as the media, police, administration, NGOs and civil society to tackle this problem in the region. Diocese of Patna, CNI in January 2008 in Patna, Bihar, organized a Consultation on "Tackling newer emerging vulnerabilities leading to trafficking in children and women in Bihar". Recently, the Church has been seriously engaged in the anti-trafficking crusade since many of its dioceses are in its sting. Its mission to prevent, protect and rehabilitate the victims requires that organized fellowship like Diocesan Women's Fellowship for Christian Services enabled to build its capacity to address the issue. A national level programme on the theme "Trafficking in Women: Role of the Church" was held at the CNI Center for Human Potential Development, Nagpur in May 2009.

Catholic Church, through, Caritas India,[6] its official social service agency, cooperates with partner organizations in dioceses and Religious congregations as well as voluntary organizations to work on prevention, protection, rescue, rehabilitation and reintegration. For the past 10 years, Caritas India has focused mainly on trafficking of women, particularly from tribal areas from where hundreds of young tribal women are brought to cities with the promise of jobs. In 2007, Caritas prepared draft legislation to present to parliamentarians and scheduled a meeting of all Christian parliamentarians in New Delhi to present them the draft legislation, after which the agency will officially present the draft to the federal labour and family and social welfare ministries. The proposed legislation seeks mandatory registration of all domestic workers with an appropriate government agency. It also wants to fix these workers' minimum wages and other service conditions, such as a healthy work atmosphere, leave and pension.

India's central government faces several challenges in demonstrating a more robust anti-trafficking effort: states under the Indian Constitution have the primary responsibility for law enforcement and state-level authorities are limited in their abilities to effectively confront interstate and transnational trafficking crimes; complicity in trafficking by many Indian law enforcement officials and overburdened courts impede effective prosecutions; widespread poverty continues to provide a huge source of vulnerable people; and the Indian government faces other equally pressing priorities such as basic healthcare, education, and counter terrorism.

About 22% of traffickers are not prosecuted due to their political backing.[7] The significant problem of public officials' complicity in sex trafficking and forced labor remains largely unaddressed by central and state governments. Corrupt law enforcement officers reportedly continues to facilitate the movement of sex trafficking victims, protect brothels that exploit victims, and protect traffickers and brothel keepers from arrest and other threats of enforcement.

Thus, there is need for an integrated approach involving all the three components prevention, protection and prosecution in effectively addressing trafficking. Since trafficking is an organised crime, involving a multiplicity of actors linked together in a chain, professional methods of dealing with them are called for. Certainty and stringency of punishment of the exploiters, without any delay whatsoever, is the essential requirement for preventing trafficking. Simultaneously, the victims need to be rescued and rehabilitated. As lack of priority, time and sensitivity as well as ignorance of the issues concerned are commonly seen as the factors responsible for the present day dismal picture in enforcement, an effective networking of the law enforcement agencies with NGOs can make adequate dent in the given situation. The order of the High Court of Delhi directing that NGOs should be associated with all rescue operations of the Delhi police testifies to the deliverance capability of this partnership. Effective methods of rehabilitation, counseling, reintegration, redressal of grievances and monitoring are instrumental in ensuring that the rescued persons are not retrafficked. These initiatives by individuals and organisations, which are sensitive and committed to the cause, need to be appreciated and institutionalized.

The Church has been successful in organizing various consultations and conferences on trafficking on national and regional level. At the same time there is a need to network within the Church and Church-related organisations, in order to strengthen collaboration and coordination of different efforts, as well as with ecumenical partners in other Churches. Networking should aim at improving the trans-national assistance and protection to trafficked persons. Networking is also a tool for joint advocacy work in seeking the improvement of legislation at international and national levels and their enforcement.

Regardless of the targets and focus of the awareness raising, particular attention should be paid to the dangers of domestic violence, as this is often a breeding ground and catalyst for trafficking in human beings.

God has created women to be agents in his great plan for restoration of justice and peace. She cited examples from the Bible of Ruth and Moses who had to move from their place of residence, because God had a purpose in their lives. Therefore, women should be united in and with the Spirit of God to work and overcome problems, and not retreat from the situation they are placed in. They are to be agents to bring joy in the lives of the oppressed

NOTES & REFERENCES

1. Krishna Iyer, Justice V.R. "Gender Justice vis-à-vis Law against Immoral Traffic - A Critique" in S.C. Bhatia (ed.), *Social Audit of Immoral Traffic Prevention Act*, University of Delhi, 1988.
2. Bhagwati, Justice P.N., *"intensifying Social Action"*.
3. Facts on Asia and Country Profiles, Conference convened by CEDPA, 1997
4. A Report on *Trafficking in Woman and Children in India* 2002-2003 by NHRC. UNIFEM and ISS Project.
5. Research Study on Human Right Violation of Victims of Trafficking Conducted by Social Action Forum for Manavaadhikar
6. The Cartias Internationalist Commitment on Combating Trafficking in Human Beings - October - 2005.
7. Trafficking in Persons Report, US Dept of State - June 2009

6

Conclusion

The overall situation in context of anti-trafficking measure as reflected at the grassroots level is infant stage. "Whatever makes a man a slave takes half his worth away"[1]. Indeed, human trafficking is a modern day slavery where human beings are exploited by treating them like commodities for profit. It is contrary to the fundamental belief of all societies that people everywhere deserve to live in safely and dignity. Victims of human trafficking who comprise of young children, teenagers, men and women are subjected to involuntary servitude and sexual slavery by force, fraud or coercion. Human smuggling, especially of women and children has become a matter of serious national and international concern. Sources confirm that nearly 800,000 victims are annually trafficked across international borders worldwide and around 150,000 of them within and around the borders of South Asia alone. The fact is that after drug dealing and illicit arms smuggling, human trafficking is the world's third largest organised crime, and growing by leaps and bounds. Commercial exploitation of the vulnerable sections of the society has led to massive growth of slave trade into a multimillion dollar business. According to the FBI, this organised crime generates $9.5 billion in revenue each year.

Unfortunately, India's record of prevention of trafficking in persons remains abysmally poor. There can be no two opinions about the fact that the problem has been under-estimated and ignored in our country. As per the women and child development estimates, 3 million women in India fall prey to traficking annually in the country and 40% of these are minors. It is shameful that even as our leaders continue to bask in their election victories, the US has placed India on the second worst category of human trafficking watchlist. "India is a source, destination and transit country for men, women and children trafficked for the purpose of forced labour and commercial sexual exploitation", says the trafficking in in persons report recently released by US secretary of state, Hillary Clinton.

Despite continuing to be the most favoured destination for human smuggling, India has failed to improve its ranking again this year and has been placed on tier II watchlist. The ranking implies that though the country is making some efforts, it has failed to meet the minimum anti trafficking standards and is therefore listed with 52 other countries that are under watch for failing to tackle the problem.

The report further says that India is also a destination for women and girls from Nepal and Bangladesh trafficked for the purpose of commercial sexual exploitation. Every year 5000-7000 Nepalies girls are trafficked into India with the result that there are more than 250,000 Napalese girls and women in Indian brothels. They become easy prey to people involved in human trafficking as they are either sold by their parents or tricked into fradulent marriages or worse still, promised employment in cities only to find themselves in entertainment houses. Children from Nepal are also trafficked into India for forced labour in circus shows. Men and women from Bangladesh and Nepal are tracfficked through India for forced labour and commercial sexual exploitation to Middle East. There are also victims of labour trafficking among the thousands of Indians who migrate willingly every year to the Middle East, Europe and the US to work as domestic servants and low skilled labourers, the report says. Many a times these workers become victims of exploitation as well as physical and sexual abuse by their ruthless employers in the destination countries. Even in India itself, women and girls are trafficked within the country for commercial exloitation and forced marriage. Other purposes for human smuggling in India include forced prostitution, marriage, domestic labour and bonded labour. In India there are millions of children from poor families who are subjected to forced labour by working in factories, as domestic servants, as beggars and agricultural workers. They have even been used as trained combatants and human bombs by some insurgent groups. Rich people in gulf countries also use them in camel races. It must not be lost sight of that human trafficking is not limited to sex trade alone but also for purposes like forced labour, commercial gay and lesbian relationships, to hire wombs, domestic slavery, organ transplantation and begging as well.

Inarguably, poverty is a crucial contributing factor for the rise in human trafficking in India. At the heart of the problem also lies underdevelopment and unemployment. It needs no reiteration that a vast majority of trafficked women are from poor, landless families or belong to dalit, adivasi and low caste communities. Girs from tribal areas and poor villages are most vulnerable to trafficking in sex trade as the need for money is high for their parents. This motivates them to sell their children for paltry sums without even caring for their security. There is also a strong connection between the problem of trafficking and the girl child who faces the higher risk of being sold at birth, living as we are in a gender biased society. For example, 40% of the children trafficked in India are from within the country while 60% are from other countries. This is precisely the case with Mandala, Sidhi, Reva, Katni and other tribal majority areas of Madhya Pradesh where the number of cases pertaining to missing girls is on a high. Though they are lured by lucrative job offers and promises of a better life, the unfortunate reality is that they land in metros like Mumbai and Delhi for being pushed into the sex trade. In some places, socio-cultural practices also motivate women, girls and minors into such shameful acts. For instance, the Northern districts of Karnataka such as Bijapur and Shimoga encourage prostitution in the garb of religion by offering minor girls to gods and godesses. Karnataka, Madhya Pradesh, Maharashtra, Tamil Nadu and UP are the high supply zones for women in prostitution. Bangalore is one of the five major cities in India which together account for 80% of child prostitution in the country.

Despite the magnitude of the problem of human trafficking, India has failed to show evidence of increasing efforts to tackle the menace. Though the government boasts of working for the uplift of these tribes and underpreviledged people, it has not strucked at the root cause of trafficking as the much touted development schemes are not reaching the poor and backward classes. Even as India faces the prospect of being moved to tier III blacklist next year, most states in the country are still not combating the crime as a priority.

Though the government feels that efforts are being made to check human trafficking, many problems like lack of punishment of traffickers and low conviction rates seriously impede India's ability to effectively combat this problem. Also, some of these criminals have political connections. The complicity of some law enforcement agents with the Mafia who control the sex industry makes it difficult to apprehend such criminals.

Notwithstanding the fact that Indian constitution prohibits human trafficking and successive governments have formulated enough laws to check the problem, we lack the will to enforce them. Consequently, these laws have failed to act as a deterrent for those involved in trafficking. They know that even if they are caught in the dragnet, they can escape easily as prosecution will take years. Besides, efforts to protect the victims of trafficking are inadequate and there is no agenda for their rehabilitation. The law cannot address all of these. The society also cannot remain callously indifferent to a problem that should worry us all. It also needs to contribute its mite to ensure that such activities do not blossom and the trafficking crisis is averted.[2]

The girls from the aborigine villages and underprivileged people are the easy prey of the people involved in human trafficking. Even a small amount of money can lure these poor people to send their girl-child to work without even thinking about her security. Sometimes, even the parents knowingly sell their daughters for the sake of money and to bring up their male child. The gender biased society also drives the people to such shameful acts.

Madhya Pradesh, the heart of the country and boastfully fastest growing state of the nation where we often get the news of missing girls. Especially, in the districts of Mandala, Sidhi, Rewa, Katni and others that have tribal majority areas the number of such cases are on the high.

The girls in the age group of 12-18 years belonging to these aborigine areas and tribes are usually lured in the name of job offers and also a better life. But the fact is that these girls are being trafficked to the metros like Mumbai and Delhi and sometimes even abroad.

The biggest contradiction here comes with the fact that though on one side, the state government is showing their apathy towards the girls of these underprivileged areas by introducing many policies yet on the other side, it does not have even a bit of idea about these cases. The sources reveal that nearly 80-90 girls are missing only from the district of Mandala. The condition of the state in total is the worst. And another very astounding fact comes out is that even the Women Commission in the state, shows no concern about these cases.

When the nationwide drive is being run to stop human trafficking, the cases like these forces us to think again and again and concludes that though the governments boast their works for the development of these tribes and underprivileged people but in reality very few things are reaching the grassroot level and to the persons really in need.

But the fact which disturbs the most is the negligence of the government towards such cases of missing girls from the villages. This ultimately raises some questions which need to be answered.

1) How the gangs are being operated in a vast and diverse country like India?
2) Is there any involvement of some very high profiled personalities behind all these things?
3) Apart from the helpers at the local level, are they having any support from the higher officials in the department of police?
4) Even after much chaos on these issues by different NGO's and continuous coverage by the media, why no stringent actions have been taken till yet?
5) How these gangs are operating so smoothly and easily?

There are still many more questions but the problem is,

even though the questions have been raised, nobody bothered to find the answers. It is not only about Anita but thousands of other girls who have suffered and are still suffering. Because the main thought which controls the thinking in Indian society is: "We don't know Anita or Sunita? Why should we be bothered about her?" But in the vicious circle of this mentality everybody forgets that it is Anita today, tomorrow it could be any girl from our city, after that from our colony, then from our neighborhood and then sometimes, it may be from our home, may be one of our own family members. So this menace needs to be fought together. We need to stand and tell these people, who takes human trafficking as a game, the power of "We, the people"

A large number of people, including children, are trafficked for different purposes like domestic help, sexual exploitation, adoption, entertainment. In fact, this nefarious smuggling of children happens via well-organised networks

Trafficking of women and children from the North-Eastern states of India and its bordering countries is a serious issue, but it has so far not drawn public attention.

The result of a survey done by an NGO reveals that around 10,000 people, mostly children, are trafficked into the North-East with a good number smuggled from Bangladesh, Nepal and other South-East Asian countries. India has been identified as a source, transit and destination point in the international circuit. Most of the trafficked are engaged as cheap labour in coal mines of Meghalaya, tea gardens in Assam and in prostitution.

"The region, besides being a transit point of human trafficking, has also emerged as a destination point. We have rescued a number of children hailing from Nepal and Bangladesh in Assam and Meghalaya who were trafficked and to work as cheap labour," says Hasina Kharbhih, team leader of Impulse NGO.

According to a study conducted by Shakti Vahini (NGO) in 2006, 'Trafficking in India' reports that 378 of the 593 districts in India are affected by human trafficking. India's porous border with Nepal, Pakistan and Bangladesh are the major reasons citied for the prevalent high levels of children being trafficked every year. "Cross-border trafficking is very much relevant in the North-East, with the region sharing borders with five countries. Some large international trafficking gangs are operating in the region," she says.

It is estimated that Nepalese children constitute 20 per cent (40,000) of the estimated 200,000 Nepalese prostitutes in India. "It is estimated that some 6,000 to 10,000 girls are trafficked annually from Nepal to Indian brothels and a similar number are trafficked from Bangladesh. 27,000 Bangladeshi women and children have been forced into prostitution in Indian brothels," a Childline India Foundation report says.

The average age of girls trafficked from Bangladesh and Nepal into India has fallen over the past decade from 16-18 to 10-15 years. Due to a demographic imbalance in Haryana (850 girls/ 1000 boys), men find it difficult to find a bride. The easy way out has been through a network of touts who help men, young, old and widowed men to find wives from West Bengal, Assam and Bihar. An estimated 5,000 girls were sold in the Mewat region of Haryana. With India sharing a 4,222km border with 28 districts of Bangladesh, most of it open with rivers criss-crossing it, traffickers take advantage of this to smuggle in their hapless human cargo.

Children are trafficked for several reasons, including sexual exploitation, adoption, entertainment and sports (for example, acrobatics in circus, dance troupes, beer bars as camel jockeys); marriage, labour, begging, organ trade (though only anecdotal evidence of this is available); drug peddling and smuggling.

Trafficking of children usually runs through well organised networks. Family, relatives, friends, community leaders, brokers, the pimps and owners of brothels, the police, political connections and the criminal nexus - all or any of these have been found to be involved in the process of child trafficking.

Images of guns, drugs and rebels have long defined India's troubled northeast. Now, a study across eight states in this resource-rich, infrastructure-poor, conflict-scarred region seeks to highlight a new worry: the rising tide of human trafficking - mostly women and girls - and its potential for hastening the spread of HIV/AIDS

India's northeast is home to 200 of the 430 odd tribal groups in the country. The region is also socially and culturally distinct from mainstream India. Along with Kerala, this pocket is the bastion of Christianity in the country.

The seven-month long study carried out by the Nedan Foundation, an Indian NGO working in the largely isolated region, was sponsored by the United Nations Development Programme (UNDP) and is expected to be released soon. "Poverty and conflict are fuelling trafficking in the north eastern states. This opens up huge possibilities for the spread of HIV. It is high time programmes address the problems," Digambar Narzary, head of the Nedan Foundation, said. "We visited 25 relief camps of internally displaced persons [IDPs] in Kokrajhar in Bodoland Territorial Council, Assam [state]. Nearly 200,000 people are living in these camps without proper food. Traffickers carry out recruitment drives in such relief camps. They make false promises of jobs as domestic help in big cities," he said.

An influx of migrants over the past few decades into northeast India from neighbouring areas has sparked ethnic conflicts over land, leading to demands for secession and political autonomy.

Many armed insurgent groups are active in the region and blood feuds are common. In the last few decades, violence has ravaged the states of Assam, Manipur, Nagaland, Tripura and Arunachal Pradesh. Assam, Manipur and Tripura have also witnessed massive displacement. Economic liberalisation launched in the early 1990s is yet to impact on the northeast in the same way that it has touched other parts of India.

Narzary noted that more than 100 young women had gone missing from the camps over the past two years. Regional analysts fear that such "missing girls" may have been sold into sexual slavery or "temporarily married" - often a euphemism for prostitution.

The fear is that many such girls are extremely susceptible to HIV/AIDS and that many have already been infected. "Young girls and women from poor, desperate families are dually vulnerable: to being trafficked into the sex trade and to catching HIV. But there are no initiatives at present to address these twin problems," Nazary said.

India now holds the second largest absolute number of HIV infections in the world, UNAIDS has said. With more than 5 million people living with HIV in the adult population in 2004, India accounts for almost 13 percent of global HIV prevalence.

Kokrajhar is one of several hot spots in conflict-ridden northeast India. Since the late 1990s, hundreds of thousands of people have been displaced in the region by regular clashes between various militant and tribal groups.

Estimates of IDPs in northeast India due to prolonged insurgency remain scarce. The Norwegian Refugee Council (NRC) said up to 200,000 people were displaced in 2003 in Assam state alone and a further 15,000 in neighbouring Tripura state. But with little reliable research, the trafficking problem is more widespread in the region than previously thought. Interviews by Nedan's field teams with 60 teenage sex workers at Dimapur, a border town in the north eastern state of Nagaland, revealed that many of the girls had been trafficked from the Naga countryside with false promises of sales jobs in big cities.

Most of the girls were from broken families, having lost one or both parents in the region's protracted ethnic conflicts. Almost all had dropped out of school and faced a bleak future, the foundation discovered.

Sexual transmission is driving India's AIDS epidemic, according to UNAIDS. This route accounts for approximately 86 percent of HIV infections in the world's second most populous country. The remaining 14 percent are through blood transfusion, mother-to-child-transmission and injecting drug use, particularly in north eastern states and some metropolitan cities.

The overall situation in context of North East Region the anti-trafficking measures as reflected at the grassroots level is infant stage. International and national level action and the activism of the Civil Society have brought the issue of trafficking under greater policy focus and executive and judicial direction, apart from enhancing the degree of social awareness about it. However, the measures taken by the State Governments are mainly focused on rescue and rehabilitation. Involvement of the States with the NGOs has so far been ad hoc in nature. Investigations have often been confined to the demand areas. Partnership between law enforcement, welfare and Civil Society organizations has not come under any significant degree of institutionalization. The traffickers manage to evade the arm of law and the trafficked continue to get abused, criminalized and punished, not to speak of the latter's re-trafficking. The strong net-working bring concerted efforts within state and community need to be established. The Panchayats/ Village Development Council/ Customary laws should play vital role in prevention of trafficking women and children from the respective villages and town in the North East Region.

The study has brought to light that trafficking, thought not reported from many places, is happening almost everywhere. The situation is worse in areas which are underdeveloped. It emerges from the study that trafficking of women and children from the North-Eastern state of India and bordering countries, in both directions, is a serious issue which has not drawn extremist activities as well as the ethnic clashes and conflicts between several groups in this region have made women and children in the entire region highly vulnerable. Lack of infrastructural development and livelihood options have exacerbated the situation. Since trafficking in this area cuts across different states and countries, it needs to be studied in details and dealt with appropriately by the agencies of the Government of India, along with the state government and appropriate NGO working in this field.

The common perception, that the rescued survivors and those who are still in brothels are 'prostitutes' who indulge in soliciting and make profits in this 'trade', has been thrashed by uncovering the reality of the situation- these helpless women and children are victims of grave human rights violations having been trafficked by vested interests by lure, deceit, compulsion, threat, coercion and, thereafter, pushed into the world of commercial sexual exploitation or other types of bondage. According to the study, the exploitation of women and children takes place not only before trafficking, but also during trafficking and after trafficking. Vulnerability situations and gender discrimination, which prevail in society, have not only been promoting and facilitating trafficking but also been perpetuating it. The rights of the trafficked person are violated with impurity. They are subjected to physical and emotional harm - from sexual assault to economic deprivation and violation of human dignity. The post trafficking scenario finds the victim at the end of the tunnel with almost no hope of survival. She is subjected to different types of conceivable and inconceivable acts of perversion and exploitation.

The study has brought out the fact that law enforcement, in most places, violates the rights of victims. It is a common practice to arrest, charge sheet, prosecute and convict the trafficked victims, human rights violations are rampant during the rescue and post rescue efforts. Hence there is a need for radical change in the law enforcement practice and methods.

The legal system of India has mostly emerged from the British system, but the specific laws relating to trafficking for commercial sexual exploitation are from the post independence era. The law enacted in 1956 for suppression of Immoral Traffic was amended in 1978 and later in 1986 when the orientation was changed to prevention rather than suppression. The amended law takes into consideration the international conventions that existed then and provides for stringent punishment for procurement, commercial sexual exploitation, running brothels and related exploitative activities. There is enhanced punishment for offences against children. It provides for closure of brothels, externment and surveillance of exploiters, etc. The Indian Penal Code also provide for punishment for rape, and selling, buying or importing girls. However, under the existing system of jurisprudence, the prosecution has to prove the case against the offenders beyond reasonable doubt. This puts a lot of pressure on the victims to convincingly present their case and substantiate the same during the cross - examinations. Absence of victim protection programmes, lengthy court proceedings, heavy backlog of cases pending trial and a lots of implementation discussed in the previous chapter on the legal regime create a situation where it is the victim who often gets victimized. Taking care from such rampant human rights violations, this study has come up with certain suggestions for the amendment of ITPA as well as for changes required in law enforcement and justice delivery.

For many of the trafficked girls, the end point is the brothel, for boys it can be a workplace where their helplessness can be exploited by putting them to hard labour on nominal or no wages, and bad work conditions. In many cases, involvement of family members in trafficking creates a very difficult situation. The study shows that even women (sometimes related to the girl child) are involved in trafficking. However, the men involved in trafficking are the main beneficiaries. They provide the muscle power and work out the strategies for the most profitable disposal of their 'merchandise'. From home to the destination point, the child passes through many a hand. There is a chain of traffickers who exploit the children en route and instill fear in their minds through threats and punishments so that the child becomes submissive and accepts all orders.

The clientele who visit the victims in the brothels are from different walks of life. Most of the clients look for girls who are young virgins and would withstand all types of perversions in silence. The strategies for action against the clientele have to be oriented according to the type of the client. Law has to be ruthlessly enforced against those who come with the deliberate intention of exploiting children and women. While their criminal activities of rape, unnatural offences, etc., have to be dealt with firmly, there is also a need to counsel young teenagers who are mostly misdirected or disoriented.

Places where the demand comes from are mostly urban, and supply areas are mostly rural or semi-urban. However, a percentage of the supply is from within the exploitative surroundings, as is the case of the children of trafficked victims and children of women in brothels. The brothel atmosphere, as revealed by the victims and survivors, shows extreme levels of exploitation. The trafficked persons have no say over the timings, the number of clients or the type of clients. They have to surrender to the whims of the clients even in matters of safe sex, like the use of condoms. The money earned by the victims inevitably goes to the brothel owner and it is upto the latter to decide the mode and timing of sharing it. Often, the victims have to take loans from the brothel owner for various personal expenses.

That trafficking is a low-risk and high-profit venture has been proved by this study. A well established trafficker with many links may easily have an extremely profitable and safe business of trading in women and children, with an income running into several lakhs a year. As far as the trafficked persons are concerned, their earnings are a pittance compared to those of their exploiters. The failure of the law in arresting exploitation in the brothels has emerged clearly. Child were used for domestic labour, industrial labour, agricultural labour and in the entertainment industry (viz. circus, camel jockeying, etc.). In the course of this study, it was found that children had to leave their studies at a very young age and this is an important factor in their becoming vulnerable to traffickers. Of the children who were interviewed, 34.3 per cent could not continue studies due to poverty. Another dimension of the problem is seen from the fact that a majority of the victims trafficked for labour and servitude are children from marginalised sections of society.

Trafficking of children, even for non-sex-based purposes, emerges as an organised affair, with the traffickers often indulging in mass trafficking. Besides the linkages of the traffickers with the source areas, the vulnerability of the victims and lack of attention by the government agencies, the culture of silence prevalent in the community has also been a factor which helped the traffickers to indulge in trafficking of children for non-sex-based purposes. The study also shows that even these children are subjected to high levels of exploitation.

The study has shown that trafficking of children for labour and servitude is also a 'business' with high profit and low risk. This research, despite being focused on the processes involved in trafficking, has provided adequate inputs to understand the variety and dimensions of non-sex-based exploitation. Though this type of trafficking is primarily for labour and servitude, the victims were not free from sexual exploitation, in addition to physical and verbal abuse. Instances are aplenty where children, both boys and girls, were trafficked for domestic labour, agriculture labour, industrial labour, etc.

Technological advancements, especially in the IT sector, have been capitalised by peadophiles who form a major constituent of sex tourists. Cyber pornography has exacerbated the scope and extent of sex tourism. This research indicates that there has been phenomenal increase in sex tourism in several cities in India. This includes the famous tourist destinations on the western and eastern coasts as well as several inland tourist spots. There is high demand of women, especially girl children in and around the places of pilgrimage, especially during festivals.

On the whole, there is hardly any awareness or any conscious effort to address the issues concerned. To top it all, there is total lack of coordination among the agencies concerned. For example, the activities of known paedophiles visiting the country disguised as tourists can be monitored only if the immigration agencies in the airports work in tandem with the state police agencies. Perhaps there is a need for a Memorandum of Understanding involving all government agencies and NGOs working in this field to prevent and combat sex tourism. Goa has made a good beginning in addressing the issues. The Goa Children's Act, 2003 is a state legislation which, for the first time, deals with the issue of sex tourism. There is a need for such legislation in other states where tourism and trafficking are linked. However, the enforcement of the law is more important than the law itself. Business promotion and tourism promotions cannot be at the cost of human rights violations. There is a need to ensure protection of child rights in these areas, which are highly vulnerable to child sex and paedophilia under the façade of tourism promotion. Trafficking for commercial sexual exploitation has been exacerbated by certain cultural and social practices in several parts of the country. This includes the devadasi system, of different states or certain localised areas, and community sanctioned customs like *nath uthrai*, which exists in certain places in Rajasthan. Sometimes, the induction of girls into commercial sexual exploitation is legitimised by conducting some 'religious ceremonies'. Girls are bought and sold like any other commodity and carry a price tag depending on their age and looks. The bottom line is that girl children are highly vulnerable to exploitation in these communities, mostly because the community itself ratifies the exploitation under the façade of customary practices. Though it may appear difficult, it is not impossible to break these community-sanctioned barriers and provide succour and relief to the women and children trafficked for such exploitation, and also prevent such instances.

The research shows that the situations with respect to the implementation of the law leave much to be desired. More than the law, it is law enforcement and justice delivery which are problematic. There is a wide gap between the number of crimes taking place and those registered in police records. This gap needs to be addressed, so that action is initiated against traffickers. Stringent action on exploiters is one of the most urgent requirements for preventing and combating trafficking. As of today, registration of crimes is usually rescue-oriented. FIRs are being registered only after rescue. The very fact that the victim has been trafficked constitutes a substantive offence under ITPA, warranting an FIR at the source area itself. Crime should be registered at the place from where trafficking takes place. If this is done, there is no doubt that more FIRs will be registered in the source area as against the demand/rescue area. This calls for proactive law enforcement, intelligence gathering, public cooperation and community policing.

The all-India pattern of law enforcement thus shows that the rights of the trafficked victims are being violated with impunity. The situation gets further confounded when these victims are the ones who get convicted. As per the Indian legal system, the court has got judicial discretion to drop the charge by discharging or acquitting the case, if there is even reasonable doubt that innocent persons have been prosecuted. Moreover, the court has powers to refer back the matter to the police for further investigation if it is perfunctory or incomplete. The court also has powers to frame the charges under different sections of law than those mentioned in the police report. Despite these provisions, as the research revealed, the victims who are charged with soliciting are the ones who are getting convicted. Therefore, the scenario of victimisation of the trafficked persons in the process of justice delivery, usually noticed in most places, exacerbates the violations of the rights of the very victims.

Issues of children tend to get neglected or ignored as they are clubbed with the issues of women. Though there are many common points, the fact that children are highly vulnerable and are the most exploited section, demands higher priority for them. All polices, programmes and activities should have a special component, separately addressing child trafficking.

One important problem I would like to brought to light is that of children born in brothels. Obviously, they cannot but be affected by the vicious atmosphere of the brothel. They are ready material for trafficking. It is, therefore, imperative that a plan, to ensure a proper atmosphere for their growth, is implemented at the earliest.

Considering the violation of rights and untold miseries that the trafficked victims have to face before, during and after trafficking, and the victimisation that results from distortions in law enforcement and justice delivery, it has been well acknowledged that prevention is the best strategy. The 'business' in women and children generates enormous profits. The demand for the services of the victims has been expanding rapidly with increasing urban incomes. As a consequence, the number of places other than brothels in urban areas, specially in metropolitan towns, where these 'services' are made available, is on the increase. All these factors emphasise the importance of prevention. The study shows that the village is usually the starting point for trafficking of women and children. The end point could be within the same state in which the village is located or another state or even another country. The victim of trafficking is a complete stranger to the place where she is brought to and may not even know the language spoken there.

These exacerbate the vulnerability of the women/girl child for further exploitation. Therefore, trafficking of women and children has to be addressed in the specific context of the push factors in the concerned community. Since the exploiters take advantage of the helplessness of poor rural families, preventive action must necessarily involve empowering the powerless, especially in rural areas.

The study has confirmed the need for an integrated approach involving all the three components - ?prevention, protection and prosecution -?in effectively addressing trafficking. Since trafficking is an organised crime, involving a multiplicity of actors linked together in a chain, professional methods of dealing with them are called for. Certainty and stringency of punishment of the exploiters, without any delay whatsoever, is the essential requirement for preventing trafficking. Simultaneously, the victims need to be rescued and rehabilitated.

The situation in the country presents a picture of lack of cohesion and coordination. Whether it is intra-state trafficking, inter-state trafficking or trans-border trafficking, the agencies involved in rescue do not seem to have any coordination with the agencies concerned with rehabilitation. The issue of missing women and children has been seen in isolation and was never seen in correlation with trafficking. There is no common platform linking up prevention strategies between source and destination areas. The absence of a national coordinating/monitoring agency has been a serious impediment in justice delivery and protection of human rights.

The number of non-governmental organisations working in the field has increased enormously during the last few years. However, the vast majority of them are located in urban centres and very few have grassroots connections. Therefore, there is a tendency among some NGOs to come to conclusions on the basis of unconfirmed reports. There is a dire need for genuine and concerned NGOs to work on anti-trafficking in the rural areas, especially in the source and transit areas. Their synergy with the PRIs, as stated earlier, can yield good dividends. Moreover a study of the functioning of the NGOs shows that they are mostly working on rescue and post-rescue activities, including protection and prosecution. There are very few NGOs which are focussed on prevention of trafficking. This area also craves for attention by the civil society.

Whether it is trafficking of males or females, there is an overt and explicit demonstration of subordination of the vulnerable by the powerful. This power could be due to the exploiter's position of authority, economic well-being, social 'status', or sheer manifestation of a criminal mind. In the case of trafficking of children for labour and servitude, it is the ignorance and innocence of the children that is mostly exploited. As regards trafficking for commercial sexual exploitation, the power equations have the additional dimensions of gender bias, female discrimination and the culture of patriarchy, which are explicit in the social systems. For most of the victims, it is a crude manifestation and demonstration of male authority and power, whether of the traffickers or the clients. Therefore, the bottom line in trafficking is the exploitation of the powerless by those in power or those who can command power, even temporarily. No doubt, the connivance and complexity of the authorities exacerbate the situation

Irrefutable is the fact that trafficking in children represents the ultimate violation of human rights and child rights. The innocence and ignorance of children have been trampled upon by adults, both male and female, for satisfying their greed and lust. The high demand for male children to be used for labour and servitude is propelled by the fact that the rights of the children can be violated without any protest or accountability. The rights of these children are violated not only with respect to working hours, work conditions, comforts and perks, but also with respect to the very fundamental issues of children's growth, development and freedom. They are not only kept captive but also deprived of their basic natural right to grow and develop ?physically and mentally. The case of trafficked girl children is still more precarious. They are victims not only of rights violations, but also gender discrimination and a host of related social problems.

At the end I would like to repeat again that to address the issue of human trafficking in a holistic and right based manner. By this I mean a correct and sensitive approach that takes into account several aspects such as right to life; right to security; right to privacy; access to health services; right to self determination on of the trafficked persons and addresses the core issue of prevention, protection and prosecution so as to bring about determined effort to prevent trafficking.

Hope this humble effort of mine results in the protection of rights of even a single child or women in the entire country I would consider my effort to have been worth while.

NOTES & REFERENCES

1. http://www.onlinewomeninpolitics.org/newsfolder_July0509/2.%20Human%20trafficking%20in%20India.doc

2. http://www.centralchronicle.com/viewnews.asp?articleID=9042

Bibliography

Books and Reports

Abraham, Shailaja. 2001. *Going nowhere: Trafficking of women and children in international sex trade*, Volume I and II. New Delhi: Dominant Publishers and Distributors.

ADB. 2002. *Combating trafficking of women and children in South Asia: Nepal report.* Asian Development Bank.

ADB. 2002. *Combating trafficking of women and children in South Asia: India report.* New Delhi. Asian Development Bank.

Adenwalla, Maharukh. 2000. *Child sexual abuse and the law.* Mumbai: Indian Centre for Human Rights and Law.

All Bengal Women's Union. 2000. *Cross-border trafficking and its impact on women and children: Proceedings.*

Amnesty International. 2001. *Claiming women's rights: The optional protocol to the UN women's convention.* London: International Secretariat.

Anti-trafficking Network. 2001. *Report of the 2nd world congress.* Dhaka.

Apte, V. and K.M. Lata. 1997. *Child sexual abuse, a hard look at the arena: Perspective in social work.* Vol.12,No.2, May-August 1997.

Armour – A directory of agencies protecting children and women against child sexual exploitation and trafficking. Mumbai: Prerana.

Arputharaj, Williams. J (ed). 1991. *An anatomy of the girl child: Campaign against the right of a girl child.*

Asia Watch and Women's Rights Project. 1993. *Modern form of slavery: Trafficking of Burmese women and girls into brothels in Thailand*. Human Rights Watch.

Asian women's fund. November 25-27, 2003. International trafficking in women: Anti-trafficking law in Asia. Tokyo, Japan.

Association for Community Development (ACD). 1995. *International migration: A study on causes and consequences,* Bangladesh: Rajshahi.

ATSEC. 2001. State level workshop held by Bihar. UNIFEM.

ATSEC. 2001. National consultation on trafficking and sexual exploitation of children. 28 to 29 July. Kolkata: ATSEC.

AWARE. 1997. *Commercial sex workers of Andhra Pradesh.* Delhi: National Commission for Women.

Azim, S. 1998. *'The girl child in crisis'*. New Delhi: Indian Social Institute.

Badal, Ramesh. 2003. *Baideshik rojgar sambandhi kanuni prabadhan* (Legal Provision on Foreign Employment). Kathmandu: WOREC.

Bajpai, Asha. 2003. *Child rights in India, law, policy and practice.* Delhi: Oxford Publications.

Bales, Kevin. 1999. *Disposable people: New slavery in the global economy.* California: University of California Press.

Bales, Kevin. 2004. *Disposable People: New Slavery in the Global Economy* (revised edition with a new preface,): University of California Press.

Bangladesh National Women Lawyers Association. 1997. *Survey in the area of child and women trafficking*. Dhaka: BNWLA.

Barse, Sheela. 1996. Child victims rights: International conference on child sexual abuse, victim protection, Investigation and trial procedure. 22-24 February. Bombay: Neerguarv Foundation and Friedich Naumanm Stithung.

Barse, Sheela. *Child sexual abuse, assault, exploitation and slavery* - A user's handbook. Mumbai: Neelgaurav Foundation.

Basu, Aparna and Bharti, Ray 2003. *Women's struggle - A history of the all India women's conference 1927 -2002*. Delhi: Manohar Publishers and Distributors. 77 -81.

Beeks, Karen D. and Delila Amir, eds 2006. *Trafficking and the Global Sex Industry* : Lanham, MD: Lexington Books

Bedi, M.S. 1992. *Protection of women in moral danger: A study of trafficking in women in Rajasthan*. Udaipur: Himanshu Publications.

Belbase, Narayan., Mona, Adhikari, and Shrestha. 2001. Judicial gender equality, education and human rights: Broadening the spectrum. New Delhi: Sakshi and UNIFEM.

Beotra, B.R. 1999. *Immoral traffic* (prevention) act, 1956 (with state rules). Delhi: The Law Book Company (P) Ltd.

Bertone, A.M. 2000. *Sexual trafficking in women: International political economy and the politics of Sex*. Gender Issues.

Bhagat, Achal. The sounds of silence - A manual for forming therapeutic relationship. New Delhi: UNIFEM & Saarthak.

Bhatia, S.C. (ed). 1988. *Social audit of Immoral traffic prevention act*. Delhi: University of Delhi.

Bhattacharya, Manjima. 1998. *Trafficking in South Asia: A conceptual clarity workshop*, 29 July to 1 August 1998. New Delhi: Jagori.

Bhoruka Public Welfare Trust. 2001. *A study on cross border girl trafficking*. Kolkata.

Blanchet, Thérèse. 2002. Beyond boundaries: A critical lock at women labour migration and the trafficking within. Dhaka: USAID.

Burra, Neera. 1995. *Born to work - Child Labour in India*. Delhi: Oxford University Press

Butterflies. Phenomenon of substance abuse and sexually transmitted diseases among street Children. Undated.

Center for Development and Population Activities. 1997. Girls' rights: Society's responsibly, taking action against sexual exploitation and trafficking. New Delhi: CEDPA.

Central Advisory Committee on Child Prostitution. 1994. *Child prostitution – In the twilight?* A status of action report. New Delhi. Government of India.

Central Social Welfare Board. 1996. *Prostitution in metropolitan cities of India.* New Delhi: CSWB.

Centre for Child Rights. 2001. *Proceedings of the Conference on Child Trafficking in India,* September. New Delhi.

Centre for Women and Development. 1996. Survey of organisations working on the issues of girl trafficking. Kathmandu: The Asia Foundation.

Chakraborty, Indrani. 2006. *Tracking our children.* A brief situational analysis on the trend of migration, child marriage and trafficking in eight districts of West Bengal.

Chakraborty, Indrani, and Lopamudra Bhattacharya. 2004. In disguise. A study on vulnerabilities in mobility, migration and trafficking in person.

Chakraborthy, Kakolee. 2000. *Women as devadasis: Origin and growth of the devadasi profession.* New Delhi: Deep & Deep Publications Pvt. Ltd.

Chhetry, Shanti. 1999. *Women Workers in the informal sector.* Delhi: Gyan Sagar Publications.

Child Pornography Racket Operated by International Tourist from Switzerland Unearthed in Mumbai. December, 2000. Mumbai: FACSE.

Child prostitution: The ultimate abuse, report on the national Consultation on child prostitution. YMCA, ECPAT and UNICEF.

Citizens Commission on Bonded and Child Labour. 1995. First national convention on freedom from bandage. New Delhi: Indian Social Institute.

Commonwealth Human Rights Initiatives. 2001. Prevention of trafficking from an Indian perspective and CHRI's initiative.

Coomaraswamy, Radhika. 2000. Integration of the human rights of women and gender perspective: Report on trafficking by the special rapporteur on violence against women: Its causes and consequences, submitted in accordance with Commission on Human Rights Resolution 1997/44, E/CN. 4/2000/68. 56th Session of the Commission on Human Rights.

Creating a Healing Environment-Vol. I. 2001. *Proceedings – Psycho-social rehabilitation and occupational integration of child survivors of trafficking and other worst forms of child labour*. Kathmandu: ILO-IPEC.

CRS. 2001. *Trafficking in Women and Children*: The U.S. and International Response, Library of Congress: Congressional Research Service.

CSED. 2002. *Child trafficking in South India: An exploratory study into the causes and extent*. Tamil Nadu: Centre for Social Education and Development.

CWDS. 2002. *Crimes against women: Bondage and beyond – Revelation of data*. New Delhi: Center for Women's Development Studies.

D'Cunha, Jean. 1998. *Prostitution and sex trafficking: A review of contemporary feminist perspectives and strategies, in Violence against women* by Shirin Kudchedkar and Sabiha Al-Issa. New Delhi: Pencraft International.

Dale, Huntington. 2000. *Anti-trafficking programs in South Asia: Appropriate activities,* indicators and evaluation methodologies, Technical consultative meeting on Anti-trafficking in South Asia. November

Davidson, Julia. Jacqueline O'Connell, and Taylor, Sanchez, 1996. *Child prostitution and sex tourism in Goa*. Bangkok: ECPAT.

Debabrata, R. 1997. *Lost childhood: The first survey of child prostitution in Delhi*. Delhi: National commission in Women.

Delhi Police and Prayas. June 2000–June 2001. Status report. Rape crisis intervention centres.

Department of Woman and Child Development and Government of India. 2001b. National policy for empowerment of women. January

Department of Woman and Child Development. 2001c. India's report on world summit for children 2000. Government of India: DWCD, Ministry of Human Resource Development.

Department of Woman and Child Development. 2001d. National charter for children. Government of India: Ministry of Human Resource Development.

Department of Women and Child Development (DWCD) 1997-98. Annual report, DWCD, Ministry of Human Resource Development, Government of India.

Department of Women and Child Development (DWCD). 2001. National policy for the empowerment of women. DWCD, Ministry of Human Resource Development, Government of India.

Department of Women and Child Development (DWCD). 2001. *Protecting children from trafficking and sexual abuse*. New Delhi: DWCD, Ministry of Human Resource Development, Government of India.

Department of Women and Child Development, Ministry of Human Resource Development and Government of India. 1998a. Situation Report on trafficking of children for prostitution. New Delhi: New Concept Information Systems Pvt. Ltd.

Department of Women and Child Development. 2001. *SWADHAR* - A scheme for women in difficult circumstances. New Delhi: DWCD, MHRD, GOI.

Derks, Annouska. 2000. *Combating trafficking in South Asia: A review of policy and programme responses*: International Organisation of Migration (IOM).

Desai, M. December 2001. *Child protection – Current status and recommendations of strategies for the India country programme for 2003-2007*. A consultancy report, Tata Institute of Social Sciences. New Delhi: UNICEF India Country Office.

Desai, Nishtha. 1997. *Paedophilia in Goa After Freddy Peat*. The Lawyers Collective, Vol 12. No. 6, 5 May.

Desai, Nishtha. 2001. See the evil: *Tourism related paedophile in Goa.* Mumbai: Vikas Adhyayan Kendra.

Deuba, Arzu R and Pinky S. Rana.. 2001. A study on the psycho-social impacts of violence against women and girls with special focus_on rape, incest and polygamy. Nepal: Saathi and SNV.

Development Dialogue. 1992. A report on the socio-economic study of female prostitutes and their children in Calcutta. Kolkata: Development Dialogue.

Dewanji, M. 1999. *Child labour problems in India – Child victims of crime problems and perspectives.*

Doezema, Jo. n.d. Who gets to choose? Coercion, consent and the UN trafficking protocol. University of Brighton: Institute of Development Studies.

Dutta, Roy and Mala. 2002. Bikiye jai: Nari O shishu pachar byabsa samparkito tadanta mulak sanbad vittik tathyabahul grantha. Kolkata: Jogamaya Prakashani.

ECPAT. 2001-2002. Report on the implementation of the agenda for action against the commercial sexual exploitation of children.

Ennew, Judith. et.al. 1996. *Children and Prostitution*: Literature review and annotated bibliograph. New York: UNICEF, Centre for Family Research, University of Cambridge and Childwatch.

Equations, APSA, UNIFEM and USAID. 2004. Rescuing child labourers: An analysis of the operation undertaken to rescue children trafficked to labour in the jewellery units in Karnataka.

Equations. 2003. A situational analysis of child sex tourism in India (Kerala and Goa). ECPAT.

ESCAP. 2003 Combating human trafficking in Asia: A resource guide to international and regional legal instruments, political commitments and recommended practices. New York: United Nations.

Facts on Asia and Country Profiles. 1997. Girl's rights: Society's responsibility taking action against sexual exploitation and trafficking. Mumbai: Nehru Centre.

Fernandes, G and Cecily Stewart Ray 2001. Raids rescue and rehabilitation. The story of Mumbai brothel raids of 1996 - 2000. Mumbai: College of Social Work, Nirmala Niketan.

Fernandes, G., F. Lambay., N. Mehta, and H., Joseph. 1994. Study and action research on the girl child in especially difficulty circumstances. India Report - 1994. Mumbai: College of Social Work, Nirmla Niketan.

Fernandes, Gracy and Cecily Stewart Ray. 1999. The Mumbai brothel raids of February, and their aftermath. (Draft version: August 20). Mumbai: College of Social Work, Nirmala Niketan

Fernandes, Gracy and N., Mehta, 1997. Impact assessment of the Bombay red light district project. Bombay: Population Services International.

Fernandes, Gracy et al. 1998. The social and health needs of sexually abused and exploited children, A study for UNESCAP. Mumbai: Nirmala Niketan College of Social Work.

Fillmore, Mary. 1994. *Women and tourism,* invisible hosts, invisible guests. Bangalore: Equations.

First Report of the Special Rapporteur on Human Rights of Migrant workers. April, 2000.

Francis, T. Miko. 2000. Trafficking in women and children: The US and International response.

Frederick, John and Thomas L. Kelly (ed.). 2000. *Fallen angels - The sex workers of South Asia.* Delhi: Roli Books.

Fredrick. John. 2002. Standards and guidelines for the care of the sexually abused and sexually exploited: Some applications for South Asia. Kathmandu: ILO/IPEC-TICSA.

Friedman, Matt. 2001. *Human trafficking: Some inconsistencies with the sections present definitions and paradigm.* Nepal: Technical

Consultative Meeting on Anti-trafficking Programs in South Asia.

GAATW 2001. *Human rights and trafficking in person: A handbook.* Bangkok: Global Alliance Against Trafficking on Women.

Gallagher, Ann. 2001. The international legal response to human trafficking. Nepal: Technical consultative meeting on anti-trafficking in South Asia.

Gangoli, G. 1998. Prostitution laws: to Legalise or Decriminalise? Lawyers Collective. May.

Gathia, Joseph. 1999. *Child prostitution in India.* New Delhi: Concept Publishing Company.

Gathia, Joseph. 2003. *Asia me deh vyapar.* Delhi Concept Publication

Ghimere, Durga. 1997. *Sexual exploitation of Nepalese girls* (with special reference to girls trafficking). Kathmandu: ABC Nepal.

Ghosh S.K. 1993. *Women and crime.* Delhi: Ashish Publishing House. 131-136.

Ghosh S.K 1996. *The World of Prostitutes* (Volume 1 and 2). New Delhi: A.P.H. Publishing Corporation.

Ghosh, Neemai and Roop Sen. 2002. Barefoot light. Kolkatta: Sanlaap and UNIFEM.

Giri, Mohini. V. 1999. Kanya: Exploitation of little angels. New Delhi: Gyan Publishing House.

Gonsalves, Lina. 2001. *Women and human rights.* Delhi: A.P.H. Publishing Corporation.

GOR and UNICEF. 1996. Report on the Survey of Children of Prostitution and children dependent on Prostitutes in five districts of Bundi, Ajmer, Jaipur, Sawai Madhopur, and Tonk in Rajasthan. Jaipur, India.

HAQ Centre for Child Rights. September 2001. *Child trafficking in India.* New Delhi: HAQ.

Haq, K. 2000. Human development in South Asia, The gender question. Karachi: Oxford University Press.

HAQ: Center for child rights. 2002. *Children in globalising India:* Challenging our conscience.

Harvey J.P. and L. Riggin. 1994. Trading away the future: Child labour In India's export industries. Washington: International Labour Rights Education and Research Fund.

Hollows, A and A. Armstrong (eds.). 1991. *Children and young people as abusers: An agenda for action.* London: National Children's Bureau.

Hossain, Amjad. 2002. Bangladesh country report for regional workshop of senior police officers to enhance cross border collaboration to stop human trafficking.

Icduygu, Ahmet and Sule, Toktas. 2002. How do smuggling and trafficking operate via irregular border crossings in the Middle East? International Migration. Volume 40(6) 2002, 25-52.

ILO. 2002. Every child counts—New global estimates on child labour: ILO-IPEC.

ILO. 2002. *Stopping forced labour.* Geneva: ILO.

ILO-IPEC. 1996. Convention concerning the prohibition and immediate action for the elimination of worst forms of child labour: Targeting the intolerable. Geneva: International Labour Organisation.

ILO-IPEC. 2001. Trafficking of girls in Nepal with special reference to prostitution: A rapid assessment. Geneva:ILO.

ILO-IPEC. 2001a. Trafficking and sexual exploitation of children: An evaluation of programmes in Colombia, Costa Rica and Nicaragua, Thailand, Philippines. Geneva: ILO.

ILO-IPEC. 2001b. Trafficking of children - The problems and responses worldwide. Geneva: IPEC-ILO.

ILO-IPEC. 2002. Unbearable to the human heart—child trafficking and action to eliminate it. Geneva: ILO-IPEC.

Impulse NGO Network. 2002. Research on girl child labour in Shillong—Emergence of a new socio-economic problem. Shillong: Impulse NGO network.

INSAF (Indian National Social Action Forum). The needs of children in Goa: Towards building an adequate response. An interim Report. Panaji.

International Bureau for Children's Rights. International dimensions of the sexual exploitation of children - Global report. Canada.

International Labour Organisation. 1996. *Child labour*: Targeting the intolerable. ILO.

IOM. 2003. Labour migration in Asia: Trends, challenges and policy responses in countries of origin. International Organisation for Migration.

IPEC. 2002. Rapid assessment on trafficking in children for exploitative employment in Bangladesh. Trafficking in Children-South Asia (TICSA). ILO.

ISI. 1993. The tribal domestic worker at the crossroads: A search for alternatives. New Delhi: Indian Social Institute.

ISI. 1995. Women in the informal sector: Multi disadvantages of domestic workers. New Delhi: Indian Social Institute.

Iyer, G (ed.). 2003. *Migrant labour and human rights in India*. Delhi: Kanishka Publishers.

Jagori. 2001. Migration, trafficking and sites of work: Rights and vulnerabilities: A pilot study report of initialfindings in Rajasthan and Gujarat. New Delhi: Jagori,

Jain, S. et. al. 1991. Situational analysis of women and children in Rajasthan. Jaipur: Institute of Development Studies.

Jaiswal, Prachi. 2000. *Child Labour: A sociological study*. Delhi: Shipra Publications.

Jayaweera, Swarna. 2003. *Gender and globalisation*, commemorating Beijing, fourth South Asia regional meeting, Bhutan, 19-21 May. Delhi: UNIFEM

Jean, D'Cunha. The legislation of prostitution—A sociological inquiry into the laws relating to prostitution in India and the West. New Delhi: Joint Women's Programme.

Joardar, B. 1984. *Prostitution: A bibliographical Synthesis*. New Delhi: Inter-India publications.

Johnston, H.et al (ed.). 1998. *Trafficking in persons in South Asia*. Shastri-Indo Canadian Institute.

Jordan, Ann. 2002. The annotated guide to the Complete UN trafficking protocol. Washington: International Human Rights Law Group.

Joshi, Madhu (ed.). 1997. *Women and Children in Prostitution: Human Rights Perspectives*. Delhi: Joint Women Programme.

Kabeer, Naila., Geetha B Nambiar and Ramya, Subrahmanian. 2003. Child labour and the right to education in South Asia, needs versus rights? Dhaka: The University Press Limited.

Kapur, Ratna. 2001. Tricks and the law: Legal regulation of trafficking, sex work and migration. Nepal: Technical consultative meeting on Anti-trafficking in South Asia

Kara, Siddharth. 2008. *Sex Trafficking: Inside the Business of Modern Slavery*, Columbia University Press.

Kar, Debirani. 1995. Kolkatar nagarnati. Kolkata: Mitra and Ghosh Publishers.

Karmakar, Sumati. 2001. *Red light area: Social environment of sex workers*. New Delhi: Dominant Publishersand Distributors.

Kavoori, P. 1984. *The Santhia: A nomadic community of western Rajasthan*. Jaipur: Institute of Development Studies.

Kisan, M. 1995. Micro studies of child labour: An analytical compilation of micro studies of child labour inMaharashtra. A report prepared for Action for the Rights of the Child (ARC) Pune. UNICEF.

Krishna, S. 1996. *Restoring Childhood*. The Commonwealth Human Rights Initiative. New Delhi: Konark Publishers Pvt. Ltd.

Kumar, K.C. Bal., Subedi., Govind., Gurung, B Yogendra and Adhikar, P Keshab. 2001. *Trafficking in girls with special reference to prostitution*: A rapid assessment. International Labour Office.

Lalita & Shalini. 1998. *Women soliciting change*. ISI & JWP.

Lim, Lin Lean (ed.). 1998. *The sex sector: The economic and social bases of prostitution in Southeast Asia*.Geneva: International Labour Organisation.

Lin, Chew. 2001. Addressing trafficking in person in the human rights framework. Asian Human Rights commission

Lingam, L. 1995. *Women in migration - A study among low-income Andhra migrant households in Bombay*. Mumbai: Women's Studies Unit, Tata Institute of Social Sciences.

Mahendra, S., Bhattarai, Vaishali., Pankaja., Dahal., R, Dilli and Crowley, Siobhan. 2001. Community perceptions of trafficking and its determinants in Nepal, Horizons. The Asia Foundation.

Maiti Nepal. 2001. *Cops unearth another child trafficking racket*. January-March Vol.2. No.1.

Maiti Nepal. 2001. Crusading for eight years. 1993 to 2001. Kathmandu: Maiti Nepal.

Manohar, Sujata. 2002. *Trafficking in women and girls*. Expert group meeting on trafficking in women and girls.EGM/TRAF/2002/WP.1.

Masika, Rachel, ed. 2002: *Gender, Trafficking, and Slavery* : Oxford: Oxfam.

Mathur, K. *et al*. 1997. *Violence against women – The WDP perspective*. Jaipur: Institute of Development Studies.

Mazumdar, Ishita. 'Widows of Vrindavan' in Dr. V. Mohini Giri (ed.): *Living death – Trauma of widowhood in India*, New Delhi: Manohar Publishers and Distributors. 77-81.

Menon, N.R. Madhava. 1993. Revised draft bills with explanatory note on ITPA. National Law School.

Ministry of Welfare. 1995. Revised guidelines for adoption of Indian children. Delhi: Ministry of Welfare, Government of India.

Mishra, Lakshmidhar. 2000. *Child labour in India*. New Delhi: Oxford University Press.

Mitra, Aloka. 2000. *Prevention of trafficking in children in the red light areas*. Kolkata: Women's Waterlink Foundation.

Mocharia, Satya. *Caged lives* - A peep into the lives of adolescent girls in Chaturbhuj Sthan. Muzaffarpur, Bihar.

Mukherjee, K.K and Deepa, Das, 1996. *Prostitution in Six Metropolitian Cities of India*. New Delhi: Central Social Welfare Board.

Mukherjee, K.K. 1989. *Flesh trade: A report*. Ghaziabad: The Gram Niyajan Kendra.

Mukherjee, K.K. 1997. *Girl child prostitution in India (Policies and programmes)*. Delhi: National Commission for Women and Gram Niyojan Kendra.

Mukherji, Santosh Kumar. 1986. *Prostitution in India*. Delhi: Inter-India Publications.

Murthy, Ranjan and Lakshmi, Sankaran. 2001. *Denial and distress: Gender poverty and human rights in Asia*. Bangalore: Books for Change.

Myneni, S.R. 2002. *Women and law*. Asia Law House.

Naik, Niraj. *Sex tourism on the western coast of India*. Vikas Adhyayan Kendra.

Nair, P.M. 2002. *Combating organised crime*. New Delhi: Konark Publishers.

Nair, P.M. and Poornima, Advani. 2000. Report of the eastern regional workshop on gender and law enforcement. Patna: National Commission for Women

Nair, P.M. and Poornima, Advani. 2001. Report of the national workshop on gender and law enforcement. New Delhi: National Commission for Women

Narula, Priya and Catherine Sluggett. 2002. The campaign against sexual harassment at the workplace: A training manual. Socio-legal Information Centre.

National Commission for Women. 2001. *Trafficking*, a socio-legal study.

National Commission for Women. 2002. Study of coastal sex tourism and gender.

National Commission for Women. 1997. National consultation on sexual exploitation of Children.23-24 July.

National Commission for Women. 1997. Study report on sexual abuse of children in Goa. New Delhi: National Commission for Women.

National Consultation on Child Prostitution. 1995. *Child prostitution – The ultimate abuse.* New Delhi: UNICEF.

National Crime Record Bureau. Crimes in India 1997, 1998, 1999, 2000, 2001 & 2002. Delhi: NCRB, Ministry of Home Affairs, Government of India.

National Human Rights Commission. 1998. Mid-term appraisal of campaign against child prostitution.

National Law School of India University. 1999. National consultation on juvenile justice—Better implementation of the juvenile justice system. Center for Child and the Law, National Law School of India University.

Nav Bharat Jagriti Kendra. 2002. Bal vyapaar virodhi abhiyaan - State level workshop, 11-12 January. Hazaribagh, Bihar.

NCW. 1995-1996. Societal violence on women and children in prostitution. National Commission for Women, Government of India.

NCW. 1997. The velvet blouse, sexual exploitation of children. New Delhi: National Commission for Women.

NCW. 2001. Trafficking – a socio legal study. Delhi: National Commission for Women.

O'Grady, Ron. 1992. *The child and the tourist.* Thailand: The campaign to end child prostitution in Asian tourism (ECPAT).

Orissa state commission for women. 1997. *Exploiting children for commercial sex* - A rapid appraisal in the state of Orissa.

Panchal, T and N., Sheikh, 1997. Documentation of police case of sexually abused girls in Bombay city between 1994-95, the special cell for Women and Children.

Pandey, Balaji, Damodar, Jena and Sugata, Mohanty. 2002. Trafficking in women in Orissa: An exploratory study. Bhubaneswar: Institute for Socio-Economic Development.

Parikh and Radhakrishna. 2002. India Development Report. Oxford Publication.

Patkar Praveen and Priti, Patkar. Frequently asked questions on commercial sexual exploitation and trafficking.Mumbai: Prerna.

Patkar, P and Priti Patkar. July 1999. Intervention in the Situation of Trafficking of Children for Prostitution and Children of Prostitutes. A Six District Report of Rapid Assessment. (Ahmednagar, Latur, Nasik, Sangli, Solapur and Thane). Mahrashtra, Mumbai: UNICEF.

Patkar, Praveen. 1995. A micro-study on girl children in Prostitution in Kamathipura. Mumbai: Prerna.

Patkar, Pravin and Patkar Priti. 2002. In Search of a New Legislation against Trafficking and Commercial Sexual Exploitation. Mumbai: Prerana.

Patkar, Pravin and Patkar Priti. 2002. *Tourism Related Commercial Sexual Exploitation of Children in the Western Coast*. New Delhi: National Commission for Women.

Patkar, Pravin and Patkar Priti. n.d. Frequently asked questions on commercial sexual exploitation and trafficking. Mumbai: Prerana.

Patkar, Pravin and Priti Patkar. *Sexual Exploitation of Children and Children of Victims of CSE*. Madhyam. Vol. XIV, No.2.

Patkar, Pravin, Patkar, Priti and Sakhrani, Monica. *Trafficking and Commercial Sexual Exploitation*, International Conventions, Laws and Policy. Mumbai: Prerna

.Patkar, Priti and Patkar, Pravin. 2004. Home Investigation Report: An effective guide in Post Rescue Operation in fight against commercial sexual exploitation and trafficking of children. Mumbai: Prerana.

Penrose., Angela., Edda, Ivan-Smith and Marilyn, Thomson.

August 1996. Kids for hire, a child's right to protection from commercial sexual exploitation. London: Save the Children.

Pereira, Faustina. 2002. The fractured scales, The search for a uniform personal code. Dhaka: The University Press Ltd.

Pradhan, G. 1996. Back home from the brothels. Kathmandu: CWIN.

Prasad, K.J. 1996. Regional profile on Sexual exploitation and trafficking of Children, Society for Awareness with learning and training (SALT). Hyderabad: SALT.

Prayas & UNIFEM, WOREC & ABC, Nepal - A Report on Regional Consultation on NGO partnership in rescue and rehabilitation of the persons affected by human trafficking - South Asia.

Prayas Institute of Juvenile Justice and UNIFEM. 2001. From darkness to light: Regional consultation on trafficking of women and children and law enforcement.

Prayas Institute of Juvenile Justice. 2000. Report of the Consultative Workshop for Multi-Sectoral Response to Trafficking and Commercial Sexual Exploitation for Children and Women in Delhi. September 21-22.

Prayas. 2002. Issues and concerns of trafficking in women and children.

Puri, S.K. A sample survey done to access the awareness level in common people regarding trafficking in women & children. Patna: Prayas Bharti.

Raghuramaiah, K. L. 1991. *Night birds: Indian prostitutes from devadases to call girls*. Chanakya Publications.

Rajagopal, S. 2002. Support services to counter violence against women in Rajasthan, A resource directory.Jaipur: Institute of Development Studies.

Rayan, Chris and Michael, Hall. 2001. *Sex tourism: Marginal people and liminalities*. New York: Routledge-Taylor Francis Group. 117-134.

Raymond, Jancie *et al.* 2002. A comparative study of women trafficked I the Migration process. CATW International.

Razario, R. 1988. *Trafficking in women and children in India.* New Delhi: Uppal Publishing House.

Refugee Reports. 2000. *Trafficking in Women and Children: A Contemporary Manifestation of Slavery,* Refugee Reports, Volume 21, No.5.

Rehman, M. M., K.S. Rehman and B. Mehartaj. 2002. *Child labour and child rights – A compendium* (First Edition). Manak Publications.

Reich., B. Robert, Otero., F, Joaquin. 1996. *Forced Labour: The Prostitution of Children, Symposium Proceedings*: US Department of Labour, Bureau of International Affairs.

Roy, Sulagna. 1998. Situational Analysis of Child Prostitution in West Bengal. Consultation Meeting for Combating Trafficking of Children and Child Prostitution. Kolkata: SLARTC.

Roychoudhury, Prajna Paramita., Bandopadhyay, Geeta and Sinha, Indrani. 1995. Status Report of Kidderpore Red-Light Area (based on Part Survey). Kolkata: Sanlaap.

Rozario S.R., et.al 1988. *Trafficking in Women and Children in India.* New Delhi: Uppal Publishing House.

SAARC. 2001. Convention on preventing and combating trafficking of women and children into prostitution.

Sachs, A & D'cunha, J. 1995. *A Prostitute at Nine.* Mumbai: College of Social Work, Nirmala Niketan.

Sakhrani, M. 1998. Maharashtra Protection of Sex Workers Act: In the Name of Protection. From the Lawyers Collective. pp.8, May 1998.

Sanghera, Jyoti and Kapur, Ratna, 2000. Trafficking in Nepal: Policy Analysis: An assessment of policies and legislative measures for prevention and control of trafficking in Nepal. Kathmandu: The Asia Foundation and New Delhi: Population Council.

Sanghera, Jyoti. 1999. Trafficking of Women and Children in South Asia: A review of anti trafficking initiatives inNepal, Bangladesh and India. India: UNICEF Regional Office and Save the Children Alliance.

Sanghera, Jyoti. 2000. Trafficking of Women and Children in South Asia: Taking Stock and moving Ahead: A Review of Anti Trafficking Initiatives in Nepal, Bangladesh and India. UNICEF, ROSA and Save the Children Alliance, South and Central Asia.

Sangroula, Yubraj. 2001. *Trafficking of Girls and Women in Nepal*: Building a surveillance system for prevention. Kathmandu: Kathmandu School of Law.

Sanlaap. 1995. Progress report on KDP Red light Area: Based on part survey. Kolkata: Sanlaap.

Sanlaap. .1998. *Child Prostitution in Calcutta: A Situation Analysis.* Kolkata: Sanlaap.

Sanlaap. 2002. *Human trafficking*. Kolkata.

Sanlaap. 2003. *Child sexual abuse*. (1995-2000). Kolkata.

Sanlaap. 2003. *Child Trafficking for Camel Race and Begging*. 1995-2000. Kolkata: Sanlaap.

Saxena, Anu. 1999. Human rights and child labour in Indian industries. Delhi: Shipra Publications.

Scott, Wallach. J. 1996. *Feminism and history*. Oxford University Press. 105-151.

Shah, Vidya. 2003. Technical Paper on Gender, Vulnerabilities and HIV/AIDS. Commemorating Beijing, FourthSouth Asia Regional Meeting, Bhutan, 19-21 May. Delhi: UNIFEM.

Shalini, SCN and Lalitha, S.A. 1996. Women Soliciting Change. New Delhi: Indian Social Institute & Joint Women's Programme.

Shamim Ishrat. 1998. *Trafficking and sexual exploitation of children of children: Bangladesh Perspective,* Centre for women and children studies, Bangladesh.

Shamim, Ishrat. 2001. Mapping of missing, kidnapped and trafficked children and women: Bangladesh perspective.IOM.

Shankar, Jogan. 1994. Devadasi Cult: A sociological analysis. New Delhi: Ashish Publishing House.

Sherwani, A. 1998. *The girl child in crisis.* New Delhi: Indian Social Institute.

Singh G., Ruma, Raj, Nikhil and Sekar R. Helen. 2002. Hard labour at a tender age: Child labour in the industries in the wake of legislation. Noida: V.V. Giri, National Labour Institute.

Singh, A.K. 1990. Devdasi system in ancient India. New Delhi: H.K. Publishers and Distributors.

Singh, K.S. 1998. India's communities, peoples of India. Vol. IV, V, VI. New Delhi: Oxford University Press.

Singh, N.K. 1997. *Devdasis*—Divine prostitution. New Delhi : A.P.H. Publishing Corporation.

Singhi, N.K. 2002. Scheduled Castes Strategy for their Development: A Study of Two Districts of Rajasthan. Jaipur: Institute of Development Studies.

Sinha, Indira and Sleightholme, Carolyn. 1996. Guilty without Trial. Kolkata: Sanlaap.

Sinha, Indira and Staff of Sanlaap. 1997. The Velvet Blouse: A Study of Child Prostitution in West Bengal. Kolkata: Sanlaap

Sinha, Indrani and Roychowdhury, Anindita. 1998. Child trafficking and Prostitution. Kolkata: Sanlaap.

Sinha, Indrani. 1997. *Princess of the Night.* Kolkata: Sanlaap.

Social Alert. 2000. Invisible Servitude: An in-depth study on domestic workers in the world. Social Alert. 2000. Trafficking: On the tracks of stolen Childhoods. Belgium: Social Alert.

Somerset, Caron. 2001. What the Professionals Know: The trafficking of Children into, and through the UK for Sexual Purposes. ECPAT UK, ECPAT European Law Enforcement Group.

SOS. 2001. *South Asian Conference to Combat Trafficking and Sexual Exploitation of Children*. 14 to 17 October 2001. Goa: Save Our Sisters.

South Asia Consultation. 2000. *The Rights of the Girl Child: Review of a Decade of programming*. New Delhi: YMCA and South Asia Partnership-India.

South Asia Partnership International Commercial Sexual Exploitation of Children: A Review of South Asia-India Perspective 2001.

Srinivasan Viji. A micro level plan to reduce trafficking in girls from Nepal to India - Operation Green Light.

STV-International Human right group & GAATW. 1999. Human Rights standard for the treatment of traffickedpersons.

Subedi, Govind. 2002. Trafficking and Sexual Abuse among Street children in Kathmandu. Nepal: ILO-IPEC.

Subedi, Pushp K. 1995. Recent migration in Kathmandu municipality - Socio-demographic and economic correlates. Kathmandu, Nepal: Central Department of Population Studies, Tribhuvan University, Kirtipur.

Swarnkar, R. C. 2002. Rural Female Sex Workers in Rajasthan: A Mapping Study. Jaipur: Human EnvironmentAction Research Society.

Tandon, R.K., and K.N. Sudarshan. 1997. *Child Prostitution*. Delhi: A.P.H. Publications.

Tarachand, K.C. 1991. *Devadasi custom: Rural social structure and flesh markets*. New Delhi: Reliance PublishingHouse.

Thapar, Romila. 1966. *A history of India*, Volume I. England: Penguin Books Ltd.

The Asia Foundation and Population Council Horizons. 2000. Trafficking in Nepal: A comparative analysis of anti-trafficking intervention approaches in Nepal.

The Asia Foundation and Population Council Horizons. 2001. Prevention of trafficking and the care and support of trafficked persons: In the context of an emerging HIV/AIDS epidemic in Nepal.

Third SAARC Ministerial Conference On Children In South Asia. 1996. 'India-country report'.

Trivedi, H.R. 1976. Scheduled caste women: Studies in exploitation. New Delhi: Concept Publishing Company.

Truong, T. 2001. *Human Trafficking and Organised Crime*. WP. No. 339. The Netherlands: Institute of Social Studies.

Tumlin, Karen C. 2000. *Trafficking in children in Asia: a regional overview*. Bangkok: Institute for Asian Studies, Chulalongkorn University

Twigg, John. and M.R. Bhatt. 1998. Understanding vulnerability: South Asian Perspective. Intermediate Technology Publication on behalf of Duryog Nivaran.

UBINIG. 1996. Report of South Asian Workshop on Trafficking in Women and Children, Formulating Strategies of Resistance. 9-10 October. Tangail, Bangladesh: UBINIG.

UNDP. 2002. Layers of Silence-Links between women's vulnerability, trafficking and HIV/AIDS in Bangladesh, India and Nepal. Switzerland: UNRISD.

UNDP. 2003. *Human Development Report*. Oxford University Press.

UNESCAP, n.d. Resource guide on using instruments to combat trafficking of women and children. UNESCAP (Draft).

UNESCAP. 2002. Recommended principles and Guidelines on Human Rights and Human Trafficking. Report ofthe United Nations High Commissioner for Human Rights to the Economic and Social Council. New York: UNESCAP.

UNESCO. 2000. *Passport to Equality*. New Delhi: UNESCO office.

UNESCO. 2001. *A Cultural approach to HIV/AIDS prevention and care: A handbook for India*. Studies and Reports, Special Series No. 5, Division of Cultural Policies.

UNICEF and College of Social Work. 1994. *National Consultation on Child Prostitution*, Mumbai: College of Social Work and UNICEF.

UNICEF Regional Office for South Asia. n.d. Mapping of advocacy and capacity building materials addressing issues of violence, abuse and exploitation of children in South Asia.

UNICEF. 1995. *Child Prostitution, The Ultimate Abuse.* Report on The National Consultation on Child Prostitution. 18-20 November. New Delhi: YMCA, ECPAT and UNICEF.

UNIFEM and United Nations Development Fund. 1998. A Life Free of Violence: It's our Right, for Women South Asian Region.

UNIFEM. 1998a. *Trade in Human Misery. Trafficking in Women and Children. Asia Region.* India: UNIFEM South Asia Regional Office with UNICEF, UNFPA and UN Inter Agency Support Unit.

UNIFEM. 2000. *Progress of South Asian Women,* Accountability to the World's Women: A Series for the fiveyear Review of the Beijing Platform for Action. India: UNIFEM.

UNIFEM. 2003. Information Dossier on Human Trafficking, Commemorating Beijing, Fourth South Asia Regional Meeting, Bhutan, 19-21 May. Delhi: UNIFEM.

UNIFEM. 2003a. *Progress of South Asian Women 2003: Accountability to the worlds Women.* Delhi: UNIFEM.

United Nations. 1994. Convention on the rights of the child: Adopted by the General Assembly of the United Nations on 20th November, 1989. New Delhi: UNICEF.

United Nations. 2000. *Integration of the human rights of women and Gender perspectives: violence against women.* United Nations

United Nations. 2001. Integration of the Human Rights of Women and the Gender Perspective: Violence Against Women - Report of the Special Rapporteur on violence against women: Mission to Bangladesh, Nepal and India on the issue of trafficking of women and girls. UNESCAP.

Vayrynen Raimo. 2002. Illegal immigration, human trafficking and the organised crime. University of Notre Dame.

Vetticatil, Jose and Sunitha Krishnan. n.d. Building new hopes:

A field experience of working with children of victims of commercial sexual exploitation in the old city of Hyderabad. Andhra Pradesh: Prajwala.

VHAI. 2002. Seen, but not heard: India's marginalised, neglected and vulnerable children. New Delhi: Voluntary Health Association of India.

Virani, Pinki. Bitter Chocolate: Child sexual abuse in India. 2000. New Delhi: Penguin Books.

Voll, Klaus (ed.). 1999. *Against child labour – International dimensions and strategies*. Delhi: Mosaic Books.

Warburton, Jane and Maria, Teresa. 1996. *A Right to Happiness - Approaches to the Prevention & Psycho-Social Recovery of Child Victims of Commercial Sexual Exploitation*. NGO Group for the Convention on the Rights of the Child. pp. 15–21 and 151–164.

Women's Rehabilitation Centre. 2002. What everyone going abroad for employment must know: Information handbook. Nepal: The Asia Foundation.

WOREC. 2002. *Cross Border Trafficking of Boys*. Kathmandu: ILO/IPEC.

Working Group on the Convention of the Rights of the Child. The Alternate Report - India. 1998. New Delhi: Butterflies.

YMCA, ECPAT and UNICEF. 1995. Report on the National Consultation on Child Prostitution.

YMCA, UNICEF and ECPAT. 1995. National Consultation on Child Prostitution: The Ultimate Abuse. New Delhi: YMCA, UNICEF and ECPAT.

Young, Richard, Sankar, Sen and Helen, Chernikoff. 1996. The reality of child prostitution: Profiting from girl child vulnerability. Delhi: UNICEF.

Zachariah, K.C., K.P., Kannan and Irudaya S. Rajan. 2002. Kerala's gulf connection: CDS studies on international labour migration from Kerala state in India. New Delhi: Centre for Development Studies.

Articles

Asian Age, 1997. 'How to earn big bucks: Rent a child to Chacha', *The Asian Age*, 16 March.

Atma Darshan. 2001. National Consultation on Trafficking in Children Mumbai, 19-20 June 2001.

Barbosa, Alexandre M. et al. 1996. 'Convicted - A lifetime of paedophilia and sadism ends". Goa today.

Baria, F. 1996. 'Sexual outrage on the beach". India Today. 11 March.

Baruah, Amit. 2002. 'India signs U.N. convention on transnational crime'. *The Hindu* (Online edition). 24 December.

BNWLA. 1996. (pamphlet), 'Movement against flesh trade: Beware of the traffickers—Protect women and children." Dhaka.

Child Relief and You (CRY). 1999. '*The Indian Child*'. Mumbai: CRY.

D'Cunha, Jean. 1987. 'Prostitution in a patriarchal society: A critical review of the SIT Act'. *Economic and Political Weekly*, 7 November.

Desai, Nishtha. 2001a. 'Sacrifice at the altar of tourism", *Goa Today*. August.

Economic Times. 2002. 'Children As Slaves'. *The Economic Times* 9 April.

Forum for Women, Law and Development (FWLD), 2002. Advocacy leaflet on SAARC convention on preventing and combating trafficking in women and children for prostitution, 2002

Ganguli, Geetanjali. 1998 'The regulation of women's sexuality through law: Civil and criminal laws' *Economic and Political Weekly*, 7 March.

Ganguli, Geetanjali. 1998. 'Prostitution, legalization and discriminalisation. Recent debates'. *Economic and political weekly*. 7 March.

Hindu, The. 1999. 'They have rights too'" 18 April.

Hindu, The. 1999. 'Child trafficking on the rise.' 6 February.

Hindustan Times, The. 1993. 'Goa is India's Bangkok: Major destination for sex tourism'. 20 March, New Delhi.

Hindustan Times, The. 1999. 'Father sells son for 10 kgs of rice.' 22 March.

Hindustan Times, The. 1999. 'Where parents sell their children for paltry Rs.1000 to earn Rs. 50 a month' 19 February.

India Today. 2001. 'Deviant devils'. 5 February.

Indian Express, The. 1999. 'HC orders rehab schemes for rescued prostitutes'. 23 June.

Indian Express, The. 1999. 'Inspect rescue homes for prostitutes: HC.' 24 April.

Insall, Roger. 1996. 'Brits turn paradise into child sex hell'. *News of the World,* London. 10 March.

Jonaki. 1996. *'Child Prostitution: Sanlaap's Experience'.* Vol. 1. No.1 November, 1996.

Joshi, Madhu. 2002."The Matrix: Commercial Sexual Exploitation in India" *The Little Magazine,* Volume III, Issue 4:35 -37.

Kelly, Liz. 2001. 'From rhetoric to curiosity: Urgent questions from the UK about responses to trafficking in women'. *Asian Women,* Volume 13: 21-36.

Kumar, Sanjay. 2001. 'Despite ban, organs still sold in India' Reuters Health 9 March.

Limanowska, Barbara. 2001. 'Employed by the global sex industry'. Woman's Global Network for Reproductive Rights, Newsletter No. 73; 14-15.

Lloyd, DeMause. 1998. 'The history of child abuse.' *The Journal of Psychohistory,* Vol.25, 3,Winter.

Mac Kinnon, Catherine. 1993. 'Prostitution and civil rights.' *Michigan Journal of Gender and Law.* Volume 1: 13-31.

Mohan, Man. 1997. 'Only lucky kids return home' *The Hindustan Times,* 21t March. Delhi.

Mumbai Age. 2002. 'Anti child labour day'" *The Mumbai Age*, May 1, Mumbai.

Nair, P.M. 2002a. "Combating trafficking in women and childlren". *CBI Bulletin*, Vol. 10, No. 4, April.

Nair, P.M. 2001. 'National centre for missing and exploited children' *CBI Bulletin*.

O'Grady Ron. 1992. ECPAT *Newsletter*. Thailand.

Patkar, Priti. 1991. 'Girl child in red light areas." *Indian Journal of Social Work*.

Pioneer, The. 1997. 'NCW favours rehabilitation: Attempt to displace sex workers flayed,' by Desai, Sandesh. Prabhu. 27 July.

Pushkarna, Vijaya. 2003. 'Mercenary scalpel" *The Week*.. 3 February. Delhi.

Rajana. 1983. 'Daughters married to gods and goddesses'. Social Welfare. Feb-March. New Delhi: Central Social Welfare Board (CSWB).

Raju, S and Archis, Mohan. 2003. 'Ringmasters ran inhuman rape circus, say victims.' *The Hindustan Times*, June 17.

Ray, Nilanjana. 2006. Looking at trafficking through a new lens. Yeshiva University Cardozo *Journal of Law & Gender* 12.

Sentinel The. 2000. '*Robbing childhood of its innocence*'. 20 August, Guwahati.

Sinha, Indrani. 1996. 'Child prostitution: A discussion'. *Jonaki*. Vol.1 No.1 November.

Sharma, Sarla. 2001. 'Issues in international sexual trafficking in women', *Asian Women*, Volume 13: 37-59.

Statesman, The. 1995 'Saraikela tribal girls 'sold' into marriage.' 26 May.

Sunday Statesman, The. 2000. 'Children of a lesser god.' 17 January.

Sunday Times, The. 1998. 'Raped at 11, a whore at 12.' 15 November.

Telegraph, The. 1997. 'How green was my valley.' 13 July. As reported in Jonaki, Vol.1. No.2. September.

Sen, Sankar. 'Sex workers shift base from Kamatipura,' *Times of India*, Sen, Sankar. 14 August.

Times of India, The. 1998. "The grimmer statistics, the Bigger the Bonanza," by Jana, S. 15 November.

Times of India, The. 1998. "Child Prostitution in India." Centre of Concern for Child Labour. November 10, 1998.

Times of India, The. 1998. "My Sister is 13 and My Mother is 30, Come and Try", by Mukherjee, J. November 15.

Times of India, The. 1998. "NHRC urges center on Action Plan against Child Prostitution," by Shailendra. 25 March.

Times of India, The. 1998. "Sexual Abuse in Juvenile Homes", by Nadgaonkar, S. May 26.

Times of India, The. 200C. "Girls forced to become 'jogins' despite ban." 27 December, 2000.

Times of India, The. 2001. "First Raped and then forced to Leave Home," by Pandey, Smeeta. 11 July.

Truong, Thanh-Dan. 2003. Gender, Exploitative Migration, and the Sex Industry: A European Perspective, Gender, Technology and Development, 7(1): 31-52.

Uma, Segal. 1991. "Child abuse in India: A theoretical overview,' *Indian Journal of Social Work.*

Week, The. 2004. Hocus-Pocus Circus: Beyond the clowning and jaded glamour lies the dark face of Indian circus industry.

Website

www.ojp.usdoj.gov/ovc/publications/infores/agg2000/welcome.html

http: regionalworlds.uchicago.edu/bibliographieessaysonmigrat.pdf

http: www.een.ulaval.ca/w3/professeurs/Dessy-Pallage3.pdf

http://www.ilo.org/public/english/region/asro/colombo/download/malrep01.pdf

http://www.ilo.org/public/english/employment/gems/download/

http://www.labournepal.org/issues/migrant labour/vulnerability of migrant workers.pdf

www.kar.nic.in/dwcd/womdev.pdf

http://europa.eu.int/comm/europeaid/projects/eidhr/pdf/anti-slavery-international-traffic-report_en.pdf)

www.hri.ca/children/tents/south asia/june01.html

www.unhchr.ch/women/focus-trafficking.html

www.un.org.in/jinit/undfw.pdf.

www.ilo.org/public/public/English/standard/ipec/online campaign/home.htm.

www.unicefusa.org/ct.

www.globalmarch.org/worst forms report/would/child trafficking.htm

www.childlabournews.info

www.ecouncil.ac.cr/about/contrib./women/youth/English/traffic

www.unicef.org/newsline/02pr01.htm

www.ageofconsent.com/comments/numberthirteen.htm.

www.panasia.org.sg/nepalnet/mahilaweb/trafficking/links.htm

www.us.ilo.org/news/pkits/worstform/trafficking.pdf

www.unicef.org/programme/eprotection/focus/trafficking/measures.htm.

www.captivedaughters.org/resources/otherorganisations/onlinelinks.htm

www.unifem-eseasia.org/gendiss/gendiss2htm

www.adb.org/documents/events/2002/reta5948/default.asp

www.unifem.undp.org/public/freeofviolence/pdfchapter_4pdf.

www.asiafoundation.org/publications/rpt_othetrafnep.htm

www.december18.net/traffickingconventions.htm(legal document)

csf.colorando.edu/mail/ppn/99/msg00034.html

www.asem.org/documents/unitedkingdom/bbc_news_internet_blamed.htm

www.libmsu.edu/haris23/crimejust/human.htm

www.captivedaughter.org

www.inet.co.th/org/gaatw

www.ecpt.org

www.cwa.tnet.co.th

www.catw.ap.org

www.iom.int

www.ilo.org

www.igc.org/iwraw/publication/ww/

www.ecpat.net/eng/ecpat

www.hrlawgroup.org/site/programmes/traffic/no6htm

Index

■ ■ ■